falling *forward*

...into His arms of grace

Sandi Patty

THOMAS NELSON
Since 1798

NASHVILLE DALLAS MEXICO CITY RIO DE JANEIRO BEIJING

Published in Nashville, Tennessee, by Thomas Nelson, Inc.

All scripture quotations, unless otherwise indicated, are taken from The Holy Bible, New International Version. Copyright © 1973, 1978, 1984, International Bibles Society. Used by permission of Zondervan.

Other references are from the following sources: The Message (MSG), copyright © 1993. Used by permission of NavPress Publishing Group.

Thomas Nelson, Inc. titles may be purchased in bulk for educational, business, fund-raising, or sales promotional use. For information, please e-mail SpecialMarkets@ThomasNelson.com.

Library of Congress Cataloging-in-Publication Data

Patty, Sandi.
    Falling forward / Sandi Patty.
        p. cm.
    ISBN-10: 0-8499-1886-3 (trade paper)
    ISBN-13: 978-0-8499-1886-5 (trade paper)
        1. Failure (Psychology)—Religious aspects—Christianity. 2. Suffering—Religious aspects—Christianity. 3. Healing—Religious aspects—Christianity. 4. Christian life. I. Title.
BT730.5.P38 2007
248.8'6—dc22   2007001539

Printed in the United States of America

07 08 09 10 11 RRD 5 4 3 2

I sincerely and humbly thank Women of Faith for letting me fall into their hearts. I have truly found a home.

I lovingly dedicate this book to anyone who has fallen and thought they would never get up. Hallelujah for second, third, fourth . . . and many more chances!

contents

Foreword

"Into His Redemptive Arms"
by Patsy Clairmont

Moving ahead while being aware of the scrutiny of others is not easy. To begin anew takes a mixture of courage and humility. It also takes a growing awareness that God is on our side, that He not only has forgiven us, but He supports us during our shaky transitions. I have found that integrating the Lord's new mercies into our life walk takes time, while we are stumbling about in our humanity, trying to grasp that we could possibly be offered yet another chance.

Once we own our mistakes and our failures, the hardest person to forgive is ourselves. We meant to be more. We meant to do better. Yet somewhere along the path we veered, and Good Shepherd that He is, aware of our willful tendencies, the Lord passionately pursues us until we are safely back in the fold.

I have watched my friend Sandi make her way back, not only to the safety of God's forgiveness, but to the liberty of His calling on her life. And I have celebrated the obvious working of His Spirit in Sandi's inner life, expanding her grace, mercy, and compassion toward others.

Sandi has a heart for those who have veered and are trying to regain their footing on the narrow path—and really, isn't that all of us? How this must please the Father to see His dear daughter tenderly regard others. The pages ahead are full of vulnerability and kindness. You won't feel judged, I assure you. This book has been dipped deep in God's immeasurable love.

It's noteworthy to recognize the way we often learn how great and deep and wide the love of God is: by falling forward into His redemptive arms.

— Patsy

author's note

Dear Reader,

You and I may not have met, but the fact that you're interested in taking this journey of *Falling Forward* with me hints that we may have something in common. Though we may have walked completely different paths to get here, we each find ourselves in need of healing, in need of the big, wide-open arms of the Savior to comfort us and restore us to wholeness. I hope I'm able to offer you some encouragement and inspiration and maybe even a little understanding. So, first, I want to welcome you with a great big virtual *HUG* and an assurance: *You're safe here.*

We're going to talk about some of the nitty-gritty details of recovering from a major life crisis, and we're going to get real about how it feels to "fail" in some way. Since this book is all about honesty, I'll start by filling you in on a few details about myself. I'm sure some of you have been familiar with my name and perhaps even followed my story ever since my first album was released back in 1979. But many more of you may know nothing about me, so I'll give you the thumbnail sketch.

Throughout the 1980s and early '90s, I was a young wife, mother, and Christian recording artist, living what looked like an exemplary Christian life. However, behind the scenes I had been struggling, and by 1993 I was separated from my husband and in love with another man. Eventually, amid great scandal and the loss of my career as a singer, I was divorced and then later remarried to my husband, Don, to whom I've been married for twelve years (at the time of this book's release).

My previous book, *Broken on the Back Row*, chronicles the years from my first recording contract up through my divorce. It also covers my process of repentance, restitution, and restoration, and my marriage to Don. Another book, *Life in the Blender*, continues the story as Don and I blended our families (we have eight children between us) and began moving on from those early days of heartache and confusion. In that book, you can read about all of my children and how we manage to run our crazy household.

The book you hold in your hands is not so much a chronicle as it is a travel companion for you as you navigate your own process of recovery and renewal. I'm looking back over the last fourteen years of my life and recounting what I've learned about how to recapture life again. It is only due to the unbelievable grace and forgiveness of our loving God that any of this has been possible, and my desire to serve Him by serving others motivates this writing.

So let's just sit back with our lattés, put our feet up, and enjoy spending this time together. I am praying that as you read this, you'll find the strength and the confidence to fall forward into the loving arms of your Savior. He's waiting for you!

I'll see you there.

— Many blessings,

Sandi

1 meet my perfect family

It is God who arms me with strength and makes my way
perfect.

— Psalm 18:32

It felt so right, this moment my daughter had been dreaming about since childhood. Wasn't it yesterday she was playing princess in my white satin slip, her tiny feet precariously planted in my sparkly "stage" heels as she shuffled down the hall, an old swatch of nylon net bobby-pinned to her dark brown curls? Along with thousands of little girls throughout the ages, Anna had anticipated her wedding day, practiced it over and over in her head, and longed for it to be absolutely perfect. She'd be the perfect bride; her sweetheart, the perfect groom; both surrounded by their perfect family as they headed off into a blissfully perfect future.

The day was turning out just as she'd hoped: absolutely, positively perfect—as long as your definition of "perfect" is as broad as ours has come to be. My understanding of "perfection" has certainly changed over the last eleven years of adjusting to and enjoying a second marriage, along with our beloved blended (and sometimes, chopped and pureed) family.

As I sat in the front pew, it was such an honor, privilege, and yes, relief, to be the one sitting below the stage with my daughter as the center of attention. All eyes were on Anna, resplendent in her elegant off-white mermaid gown. The siblings and stepsiblings were lined up as attendants, the girls looking magnificent in pale sage gowns. Anna and her handsome groom, Collin, had just knelt face-to-face at the little altar to begin taking communion. Then, something happened (doesn't something *always* happen at weddings?) that became a perfect metaphor for our family. Even now, the retelling leaves me alternating between laughter and tears. No matter the outward expression, my internal emotions are joy mingled with gratitude and love, plus a generous dash of sheer astonishment at this perfectly beautiful, crazy life God wrought from the ashes I laid at his feet more than a decade ago.

What happened was that my stepdaughter, Mollie, a bridesmaid and the most sensitive of our blended brood, began to get "a little green around the gills" as they say in my home state of Oklahoma and—with another nod to an Okieism—was about to go down like the Titanic on an ocean of sea-foam chiffon.

Like a well-trained rescue squad, we automatically flew into action to help the downed family member. Don (my husband) immediately stood up to retrieve his daughter and help her down to the front pew of the church, where he knelt and fanned her with a wedding program. I positioned myself near Mollie's head, where I went into nurturing mode, whispering comfort and stroking her hair. Mollie's mother, Michelle, took a place at her daughter's feet where she massaged her legs, directing the blood toward her heart. John Helvering, my ex-husband, sent someone to get orange juice to help stabilize Mollie's blood sugar. Anna and Collin were frozen in their places, looking for all the world like wedding-cake toppers with twin deer-in-the-headlight expressions, both of them caught off guard by the family sideshow unfolding in Pew #1.

The various sibs and stepsibs watched the action, waiting for a thumbs-up that Mollie was okay. It turned out Mollie had forgotten to eat that afternoon in all the excitement, and between the heat and the adrenaline, the low blood sugar just got the best of her. Eventually she felt better and decided to remain on the front pew. Anna and Collin were not about to go on until they knew Mollie was okay, but then, seasoned recoverers that we are, everyone took their places and our daughter resumed getting hitched without, well, a hitch.

Later my friend Shari would remark, "Sandi, only God could have brought about the perfect coordination of a family that had once been so fractured." She was right. Though the picture that will go in our family album will be the one where we all looked perfectly poised, coiffed, and oh-so-together, the more precious "family photo" will be the one that the camera missed but is captured for all time in my mind. It will be a picture of the whole family, extended and intimate, working as one to help a daughter and sister in need.

Families may have their squabbles but when one of their own goes down, most of us let the small stuff go and immediately band together to retrieve and revive the fallen. A family isn't unlike the units of firefighters who went in to rescue their perishing brothers when the twin towers were hit on 9–11 or the World War II soldiers from the miniseries, *Band of Brothers*. They may have their disputes, but when it counts—when someone is wounded (either by enemy fire or by his or her own carelessness)—families, firefighters, and soldiers stand shoulder to shoulder together in their efforts to restore the wounded one.

Now freeze-frame these pictures in your mind for a moment. A daughter faints, and a family—odd though its makeup may be—moves to help her. A team of rescue workers walk into a burning, melting hell with only one thing on their mind: to save their fallen comrades. It occurs to me that perhaps this is part of the picture Jesus had in mind for his family—his church. "Greater love has no one than this, that he lay down his life for his friends" (John 15:13).

we all fall down

As I'm settling down to write a book about falling and how to do it with grace, a nationally known and highly respected leader, adviser to the president, beloved and esteemed pastor, husband and father, has been exposed in a scandal that I'm sure will rock many circles in the weeks and months to come.

If your first reaction to hearing of a big fall by a well-known person is "Wow. Thank God I'm not *that* messed up," you aren't alone. It's human nature to want to compare sins and scan your world for someone who is lower on the sin totem pole than you are. I'm not sure why, but it's easier for us to play "Let's Compare" than it is simply to look at the big log in our own eye and experience the gratitude that comes when we know that Jesus still loves us just as we are, telephone pole protruding from our baby blues and all.

More and more I well up with tears of thankfulness when I come across Christ-followers who don't act shocked or appalled when a Christian turns out to be a fully human sinner, but who, instead, simply roll up their sleeves and dive in, doing what healthy families do in times of crisis.

As perhaps most of you will know, I fell off the proverbial wall due to my relationship with Don, my current husband, while I was still married to my first husband. Both of us were in places of pain and vulnerability that only Christ knows about—but we were both married, and there was no excuse for violating our vows. The affair was wrong, wrong, wrong, and I won't try to offer up reasons or excuses. Sin is sin, period.

I was trying to be "Miz Perfect Little Thang" before that Big Ugly Fall, so the experience was accompanied by enormous public shame and a singing ministry/career that went down the tubes for nearly a decade. By God's grace, a family who tended to my wounds, and the King's finest men and women bringing me spiritual, emotional, and physical help, love, healing, and accountability—I was put back together again. Though I'd do anything to erase the sin that led to the fall and the hurt left in its wake, I have to be honest with you: I like the Sandi that's finally landed on this side of the wall, in her Father's arms, better than the old Sandi.

5

This Sandi has been broken, but she's more compassionate to others who struggle in a wide variety of ways. Whether you are wrestling with deep woundedness from childhood, or one of the Top Ten Bad Sins that have huge consequences, or a marriage that just doesn't seem to work right, or the daily effort to have more patience with a two-year-old who's just smeared peanut butter on your last nerve—I'm not writing with stones of judgment in my pocket. I come with a cool cloth, a glass of juice, and a boatload of compassion.

Interviewers sometimes ask me what I want to do with my life now that I'm restored, healed, and happy. I'll tell you plainly: I want to be an encourager—through my songs, my words, and my life—to others who are faltering, stumbling, or have already fallen. I want to be the friend who draws closer rather than recoils when someone confesses their personal struggles. I want to embrace the sister who is facedown in the muck of her life and remind her she is as loved by God right now as she ever will be or ever has been.

I know, really *know*, that given the right emotional wiring, a painful background, temptations galore, and past traumas plus a severely fallen nature, I am capable of any and all weaknesses, mistakes, and sins. In fact, when I am most aware of the bad choices I am capable of making, I am most aware of God's goodness. When I was in the New Life Treatment Center (more on that later), I met a lot of people struggling with different issues. One of the biggies was alcoholism. They used to say, "We are only as strong as our ability to resist the next drink." I realized that the concepts from AA and other 12-step programs are broadly applicable to any struggle with sin or temptation. We all carry within us the capability of making poor choices, and we are only as "well" as our ability to make the next right choice.

Henri Nouwen once wrote about this blessing of brokenness. He pointed out that at the last supper with his disciples, Jesus took the bread, broke it, blessed it, and then gave it. So, too, he implies, God does with our lives. Jesus takes us and sometimes must break us (usually to expose the yucky stuff inside that needs a good cleansing); then he blesses us after our brokenness and gives us away to a hurting world that needs more empathetic and compassionate "wounded healers" than it does airbrushed religious figures.[1] James says, "We all stumble in many ways" (James 3:2).

How do you stumble? Where do you feel you simply can't get your act together? Where do you constantly feel you fall short? Where do you feel "less than worthy" to be called "God's beloved"?

red-letter discovery

During a brainstorming session for this book, I was chatting with a couple of gals who've experienced their own particular brushes with the cement floor of life. We were each in various places of healing, though I'd had the most years of recovery under my belt. I'd just spoken and sung at the Women of Faith conference in Minnesota, and we were enjoying a bit of downtime in a hotel room on a sunny Saturday morning.

One of the women kicked off her shoes, took a sip of her coffee, leaned back on a propped-up pillow, sighed sadly, and confessed,

"I sometimes feel like I'll always go around with a scarlet *A* on my chest."

I nodded, as I, too, know the heavy burden of feeling eternally labeled as "That Famous Christian Singer Who Sinned Big-Time."

Then she continued, "Yesterday as I was trying to take a nap, I was so tired, but sleep wouldn't come. Then this clear mental image floated into my mind, and I can't help but wonder if it was God's message of encouragement—not only to us, but to all women who feel unworthy to hold their heads up as God's daughters. In my mind I saw every one of the thousands of women at the convention center this weekend wearing a scarlet letter *A* on her chest. Sometimes the *A* stood for *adultery* but other times it stood for *abortion* or *anger* or *addiction*. Some stood for *abuse victim,* some were branded with *anorexia* or *appetite,* and some wore the label of *abandoned.* I realized it isn't just the big public failures that weigh us down as women. We're all sporting some sort of invisible label that feels heavy on our hearts."

"Isn't that interesting?" I commented, curious.

"Yes, well, it gets even more interesting. As I got a closer look, I could see that the *A* on every woman's chest actually stood for *atoned*—which means *paid for in full*—and that the letter was scarlet because it was written in Christ's blood."

At this point, I threw up my hands and said, "That is amazing! What a beautiful picture of *grace.* If we could only see what God sees, we'd hold our heads up and be free!"

Later I shared this image with my wild and wonderful partner in crime . . . er . . . I mean *ministry*, Patsy Clairmont. (If you've not seen Patsy on stage with me in her black "Blues Brothers" shades, belting out "Ain't No Mountain High Enough," you've simply missed one of life's most exuberant summits.) Funny as Patsy is, she also has a deep contemplative side that I've come to cherish. She told me later that week, "I couldn't get that image of the letter *A* out of my mind." I began to feel more and more that this picture was indeed a little heaven-sent message for us.

In Hawthorne's original story of *The Scarlet Letter,* readers get a glimpse at the human struggle behind the public sinner/adulteress. The beloved behind the label. The struggle before the sin. In other words, we get a sneak peek at what God sees—the whole picture. For every headline you read about someone; for every person who signs in at a psychiatric ward; for every recovering addict who has introduced herself or himself at a meeting with the words "My name is ____ and I'm a ____;" for every average person who has said, "I just blew it royally with my kids, my husband, my friend, my diet;" there's a story that started from birth and led to the chapter she or he is currently surviving. Perhaps the good news of the gospel is this: "Your story isn't finished yet. With God's grace, my dear child, the best is yet to come."

perfection revisited

As long as I'm confessing, I'll let you in on something else: For much of my life, I had a real problem with Matthew 5:48, "Be perfect, therefore, as your heavenly Father is perfect." If this is what it means to be a Christian, honestly, it pretty much disqualifies me and everyone else. Then one day I read an essay by Stephen Arterburn in the *Spiritual Renewal Bible*.[2] He explained that the word "perfect" is *teleios* in the original language and that it has several meanings. I perked up right away. One definition is "completion," and another is "the appropriate stage at the appropriate time." For instance, a tree that has no leaves in winter is perfect. It is at the appropriate stage for the appropriate time. *Ah, ha!* I thought. *Then we really do have the perfect family. Considering all that has happened in the past, we are exactly where we should be at this time of our lives.* We're not without fault, mind you, but that isn't what perfect means. We are in process. We are growing, blending, learning, sometimes struggling, but always loving each other.

Can we talk? (We've known each other for a few pages now, after all.) Have you ever had the following thought about someone who seemed *so together*, so perfect, so untarnished? *What she needs is a good crisis—maybe a difficult toddler or an out-of-control teenager or a financial dilemma—something that helps her understand my less-than-perfect life. If she could only admit to a struggle, I might actually enjoy being around her!* That's because going through heartache or failure refines and redefines our image of self, of others, and of Jesus in a profound way and it usually has a lovely softening effect on our personalities. Especially if we allow ourselves to *fall forward* instead of slide backwards.

And *falling forward* (drum roll please) is the central theme of this book and one of my favorite new songs. What does it mean to fall forward, anyway? I'm so glad you asked.

When I was a little girl, my father was just about the best daddy any daughter could have. (Still is.) I never remember a time where my father said, "Just a minute" or "I'll be with you later." He gave me a great picture of the heart of God by always coming the moment I called (or at least that's how I remember it). Therefore, I had a deep trust that my daddy always had my best interest at heart. One day, however, he tested this trust. My brothers and I were up on a low roof and my dad was on the ground when he asked us to jump into his arms. My brothers stood up and jumped without hesitation. Then it was my turn. I stood with my toes at the edge of the roof and could feel myself swaying, but I didn't want to jump. I was terrified. Then Daddy said, "Sandi, you're gonna fall either way. If you fall backwards, I can't help you. But if you fall forward, I'm going to be able to catch you."

That is exactly the picture I want you to hold in your mind if you are struggling in any area of your life. If you are wounded by circumstance or the betrayal of others, if you are in despair about your marriage or your children or your future, if you are being swayed by temptation, you probably feel like you are falling. Go ahead and fall, but fall into the arms of the One who can save you. Christ understands us in the same way a father is patient with his child who is learning to walk and to trust. As long as the child is facing his daddy, as long as the child is leaning toward love, falling will be a part of learning to walk, and someday to run.

I'm a huge football fan, and our son, Sam, is eleven years old and playing Little League football. We're just having a fabulous time watching him run, tackle, and catch. One thing I've heard the coach tell the kids over and over is, "When you run the ball, you're gonna get knocked down! So when you fall, *fall forward*. At least make the most of your fall. You're either going to gain three yards or lose three yards. Better to use that fall to get ahead!"

This is another aspect of falling forward, one we'll talk about more as the book unfolds: Don't waste your pain or your failures. Use them to fall forward. Learn all the lessons you can from your failings and you'll at least save yourself from stumbling in the same way again.

I want to share one last story from Anna's wedding day that I hope will encourage you. At the reception, during the part where the announcer introduced the parents, we'd originally planned to have my ex-husband walk in alone as Anna's dad, and then Don and I, her mom and stepdad, would walk in together. However, after the fainting-spell–bonding episode that had occurred a little while before, I had a wild thought.

I went over to my ex-husband and said, "I don't want you to be uncomfortable with this suggestion, but what if the three of us walk in together?"

He smiled and agreed wholeheartedly right away! So the three of us walked in together, with me in the middle, one arm linked with my current husband's and the other arm with Anna's father's. This was Anna's world, we were her parents, and the truth of that was more powerful than any of our personal issues.

John could have said, "Sandi, I'm not comfortable with this idea," and that would have been fine. But for him to say, "Absolutely!" was an indicator of how much healing has happened since those tense days (okay, *years*) when we could hardly stand to talk to one another.

It's one of those precious "perfect" things that happens over time, with heavy doses of forgiveness, prayer, and a realization that all of us kneel at an equal height at the foot of the cross.

It's the sort of everyday miracle that occurs when we falter, stumble, or fall—but somewhere in that process we make a conscious choice: to *fall forward.*

And the greatest thing I discovered [was that I could be] fully known and fully loved. Jesus knew the worst and He loved me. What a relief to know the worst about yourself and at the same moment to be embraced by God. It's so liberating to reach the end of yourself.

— SHEILA WALSH[3]

2 falling, falling, falling

Even youths grow tired and weary, and young men stumble and fall.

— Isaiah 40:30

I was raised in a home full of faith by two parents who loved each other and loved me and my two younger brothers, Mike and Craig. Most of my life I would have considered myself a "good girl"—I didn't make a lot of waves or indulge in any great rebellions. For the most part, I followed the rules. When first hearing Jesus' well-known parable of the departure and return of the prodigal son, I was among those on the Sunday school sidelines who silently *tsk-tsked* the foolish son for taking advantage of his loving father, grabbing his inheritance, and squandering it on passing pleasures. When the boy's fall into destitution caused him to sit down and dine at a trough full of pig slop, I felt only slightly sorry for him. After all, look at the choices he made! He deserved a harsh wake-up call—and probably worse.

15

In truth, I internally sided with the poor, overlooked, well-behaved elder brother. What obedient child would not be upset to watch a wayward, irresponsible sibling come back home with empty pockets and a sad sob story—only to watch Daddy not only forgive the kid, but give him a ring, a robe, and a party!

It was all just too much.

And then, of course, there came the day when I woke up in front of my own self-induced plate of suffering. Now I was the prodigal child. I was the one deservedly staring at a trough of pig slop for supper.

After I woke up at the pig sty I'd made of my life, I began my journey back to my Father's house by checking myself into New Life Clinic for two weeks. It was there I would discover that the seeds for my prodigal wanderings actually began with an elder brother blind spot. During those two weeks, surrounded by counselors who understood journeys like mine, I experienced the most amazing freedom. It astounded me how much honesty and truth were behind the locked doors of the psych ward.

It wasn't long before my counselor began to pick up on my tendency toward perfectionism. She spotted that I had great difficulty allowing myself permission to make mistakes. *Things should be perfect, I should be perfect.* Therefore, when I began to encounter "imperfect" emotions within myself, I thought there was something irredeemably wrong with me. At points when I'd automatically go into denial or apologize for "wrong" feelings, she would gently say to me, "Lean into that, Sandi. Don't brush by it. Lean into what you are actually feeling, not what a good Christian woman is 'supposed' to feel. It's okay." When I'd start to protest, she'd remind me, "Sandi, you need to lean into your true and honest emotions in order to understand them and allow God to bring healing there." Thinking back on it now, I realize that leaning toward the deepest truth of what I felt, right or wrong, was actually one of the first and most profound steps toward falling forward. By leaning into my truth, I leaned closer to the Father's embrace.

If only humans could see our sin from God's eye view! Christians would probably judge my outward sin as the worst one I've ever committed. I probably would have agreed. After all, my Big Sin had huge consequences and hurt many people. But in truth, it was the private "spiritual sin" that began my eventual prodigal slide into public pig slop, so to speak.

In talking and observing others who have landed at the bottom of their lives, I've discovered we all have pretty similar patterns. Our prodigal wanderings usually begin with elder brother ways of thinking. In my own life, it went something like this:

I am a good girl, and therefore I do not think bad thoughts or do bad things.

I am in a marriage that is so painful, I do not know what to do. But I must not stop and tend to my heart's inner cries, because my husband and my Christian public need me to be "Sandi Patti"—well-known and beloved Christian singer, wife, and mother. Like Mary

*Poppins, I must be "practically perfect in every way." (Or at least keep
up the image as best I can.)*

At that time, even my name was misspelled because of a mar-
keting mistake early in my career. Is that telling or what? I was
trying to live up to an image that was not even "me." So I
ignored the pain building up inside and continued, exhausted
and empty, in ministry because that is what I thought others
expected of me. And because I lacked the courage to speak up
for my wilting heart.

Self-imposed martyrdom can be a dangerous thing. Why? Our
wounds remain pushed down but also untended, unhealed, and
open. Then when some sort of medication for our pain is offered,
however temporary or ultimately destructive, we are less able to
fend off the temptation. Self-medication can take many forms,
including food binges, workaholism, escape into fantasy romance
novels, nonstop thrill seeking, street or prescription drugs, Internet
porn, the illicit but comforting embrace in another's arms, alco-
hol—a veritable cafeteria of "fleshly sin" offerings. But where did
these more obvious outward sins begin?

They began with pride, an "elder brother" sin, that whispers, "I
must be perfect. I must not fail. I must keep up appearances. I have
to make straight A's on this exam of life because people are count-
ing on me." Though it may come in a guise of humility, the attitude that any of us can do it all is actually, at its root, the sin of
pride. It's no wonder the Bible tells us that "Pride goes before
destruction, a haughty spirit before a fall" (Proverbs 16:18).

faltering

In tending to the hearts of other sisters who write me about their own brokenness, they are usually in one of three stages of struggling: faltering, stumbling, or falling.

To falter means to "move unsteadily; to hesitate in purpose or action."[1] It is at this point of just beginning to feel off kilter that it is easiest to receive help in the form of a steadying hand of friendship or even a good book, seminar, or extended weekend of prayer and renewal. This is why "early intervention" is always the best choice when you begin to realize you are faltering in your journey with God and others. How sisters need to reach out to each other at this point! "Those of us who are strong and able in the faith need to step in and lend a hand to those who falter, and not just do what is most convenient for us. Strength is for service, not status. Each one of us needs to look after the good of the people around us, asking ourselves, 'How can I help?'" (Romans 15:1–3 MSG).

How do you know if you are faltering? What are the symptoms that leave us especially vulnerable to a downward spiral—spiritual, physical, or emotional?

Here are a few:

Running on Empty. This happens so easily to nurturing types. In a funny but all-too-true article by life coach Martha Beck called "Overhelpers Anonymous," she says that women are particularly susceptible to getting "addicted" to the rush that comes from a helper's high. However, Beck points out that there is a downside to constantly caring for others while neglecting ourselves: exhaustion and resentment."

My friend Sheila Walsh says that one of the easiest places to hide and get our fix is the church. Nobody is going to question why you are signing up for yet another committee meeting. In fact, you'll get lots of pats on the back for being the one folks can always count on to volunteer. The church is capable of fostering an unhealthy balance—allowing us to "hide" through our overcommitments and stay so busy, busy, busy there's no time for periodic self-examination or to allow God to ask us why we are running so fast on a empty tank.

Desperate to Escape Your Current Reality. When you see a commercial on TV about getting away to a remote island, does every cell in your body yearn to do just that? We all have moments of longing to escape to paradise, but when your days and nights are accompanied by an almost ever-present, persistent urge to run away, if your daydreams get more vivid than your real life, if you find yourself routinely escaping into fantasy—you are faltering.

As one who didn't get the deep kind of help I needed at this point, let me urge you to learn from my mistakes: if you are in a place in your mind where you are feeling desperate to escape your reality—this is your *red flag*! Sound the alarm. Force a crisis, get help, do something positive and tend to your aching soul. If this sounds like where you are, and you've ignored or downplayed your feelings, I beg you to listen to your heart. It is telling you that you are in a desperate place, that you are vulnerable, and that *now*, not tomorrow, is the time to address the root of your discontent.

As I look back, I can remember the moment that I began to "wish for another life," so to speak. I was on an airplane, traveling from California to the East Coast. The flight was long, so they played a movie to pass the time. It was the comedy *Overboard*, with Goldie Hawn and Kurt Russell. It is actually a very funny movie about a woman who gets tossed overboard off her yacht, bumps her head, and loses her memory. She is very wealthy and has the attitude to go with it. When she falls overboard, a very poor family consisting of four rambunctious boys and their father (Russell) "claims" her, and she begins to make a life with them. Though there is a lot of comic trial and error, eventually she finds much happiness in her new life. And then her memory comes back. In a classic fairy-tale ending, she decides to stay with her new-found "happy" family and give up the "old" life of riches.

Sweet story, right? Well, here's the red flag that was going off in my heart at that moment. People all around me were laughing, but I sat in my airplane chair, sobbing, recognizing how much I longed for another life. I was inwardly desperate to escape my current realities.

But what did I do? I got off the plane, painted on my can-do smile, and carried on as best I could without yelping for help. I now know that the time to start signaling for help is as soon as you start having unusual and deep emotional responses to what would be to others a normal scene or experience.

Unpacked Baggage. One of the issues I ignored for many years because it didn't seem to warrant attention, was that I'd had a frightening, abusive sexual experience at age six. My parents had to go on a short singing tour. Dad sang in a quartet and Mom was the pianist. A woman volunteered to keep me in her home for a week, and since she was in my dad's choir at church and was also a school teacher, my parents thought it would work out great. I wouldn't have to miss any school, and I'd be well cared for. Sorrowfully, the woman proved to be mentally unstable and abused me in sexual ways that my little mind simple couldn't comprehend. I only knew I was afraid and deeply embarrassed.

I didn't tell my parents about the incidents, and even as an adult, when I compared what happened to me to others who'd been more severely abused, I didn't think it all that significant. But I was wrong. Any time you are sexually abused, even if it seems mild in comparison to other women's stories, you were handed some baggage that burdens your relationships. Generally women react to being abused or misused by becoming either a doormat or a bulldozer—letting people walk all over you or you walking all over people. You feel like damaged goods. Unknowingly, you may draw people into your life who are going to affirm your poor view of yourself. It feels somehow right and comfortable. (More about "baggage handling" in Chapter 7.)

stumbling

For those of us who ignored the first warning signs, the next phase of a fall is what I refer to as the stumbling stage. Once you go from faltering—or feeling internally off-balance—to stumbling, where you start tripping over your feet, it is a lot harder to keep yourself from stage #3, the actual falling. Just imagine yourself walking along, and you start to lose your balance—to falter. If you grab a guardrail or a person to hold on to at this point, it's fairly easy to right yourself.

However, once your feet start actually tripping, just ever so slightly leaving solid ground, it is much harder to get your balance again. It is even harder for someone else to catch you before the fall, because the momentum has shifted toward gravity's pull. Still, it is much better to yelp at this stage than just continue to fall headlong! You may need stronger assistance, however. Where a good friend, a helpful book, a weekend away, or some time for prayer and refocusing might help you through the *faltering* experience— when you start *stumbling*, you will probably need to call in bigger guns: professional help, a spiritual counselor with lots of experience, an extended week of in-patient counseling away from pressures of daily life, or even a rehab clinic.

How do you know if you are at the stumbling stage? Generally, you start to allow your personal boundaries to blur.

Before my fall, I was very careless with boundaries. I would innocently flirt with other men. I would have business meetings on the road in my hotel room or spend one-on-one time with men. Looking back, I realize that I had the mind-set that I was, first of all, an unattractive woman. So I never felt I could possibly be a temptation to any man. I now know that discussing deeply personal things with men automatically brings about a bond; but again, I saw myself as so unattractive, I didn't think twice about it.

When I finally verbalized to Don that I was attracted to him, I was stunned when he said that he couldn't stop thinking about me.

I've since learned that going from imagination to verbalization of feelings of attraction is a critical step that leads most people from faltering to stumbling to falling. There is no taking back words like "I'm attracted to you." That one sentence changes everything. In hindsight, I know I should have verbalized my feelings about Don to a trusted girlfriend or counselor. I was ashamed yet excited at the same time. I never dreamed that Don would be attracted to me. I couldn't believe that I would matter to anyone, certainly not any man, and not romantically.

I was also careless with strangers. When I would order room service in a hotel, I would casually answer the door in my jammies, let the room service attendant in, and close the door behind me, never giving it a thought. I would walk places that weren't safe — by myself—because again, who was I that anyone, even a would-be rapist, would be attracted to me?

I was naïve, and my self-image was so low you could have scraped it off the floor. But that was then. This is now.

Now, it is *imperative* to me that I never (or very, very rarely) meet with anyone of the opposite sex alone anywhere. If we have a meeting, we go to a restaurant or an office where there are always other people around. I make sure I keep it strictly business, and if I need to process anything, particularly emotional topics, I call my husband, my parents, or my girlfriends. When I order room service, I make sure I am always appropriately covered up, and I stand at the door, holding the door open, while the waiter brings in the food. I really try to foresee and avoid setting myself up for any situation that could be seen as a compromising position! Knowing my husband is crazy about me has helped me realize that (1) I am an attractive woman and (2) I need to do everything possible to guard his love and trust.

Here are the warning signs if you are stumbling:

Living Life on the Edge. You find yourself living more danger-ously, putting your proverbial big toe in the rushing river of self-medication. Most women who have survived a fall can tell you the very moment they put their "toe" in the water and what they did or said that opened the floodgates. One woman is fighting addic-tion to painkillers that started with a very real and chronic neck pain problem. She remembers the very first time she went to the pill bottle when her neck wasn't actually hurting. It was a huge warning sign—one she chose not to heed. Honestly, I remember thinking that I was so "thirsty" in my desert of desperation and loneliness that even dirty, gritty water tasted good.

You Become an Expert at Rationalization. At this stage of self-deception, your mind can take some incredible leaps from logic to rationalize the wrong you are contemplating and make it sound right. Many people find they go through an emotional split of sorts in their personality as they separate their lives into segments. You may be absolutely convinced that you love God, love people, and are committed to living your life for Christ. But there is this other self—the part of you that finds temptation, well, tempting.

People who are stuck at this place often talk about not being able to feel, or getting numb to life in general. When asked, "What were you *thinking*?" after being caught in some crazy dilemma, the person may respond quite honestly, "I wasn't thinking. I trained my mind to not think."

falling

Well, this isn't really a hard stage to recognize, is it? This is the place where you are:

- succumbing to temptation

- feeling powerless to get back up on your own

- experiencing powerful contradictory emotions telling you to stop and to continue on

- feeling great fear at being found out

What if you are in this place?

Then I have a boatload of comfort for you. God is everywhere, but I sometimes think He is especially near to the floor of our lives, when we mutter the most profound and heartfelt prayer that's ever been prayed by humans who are overwhelmed by brokenness or sorrow: "Please, help."

the road back to the Father

One of the most beautiful aspects of the story of the prodigal's return is that the son was given both mercy *and* grace. What is the difference?

Mercy is not being punished as we deserve. It is being forgiven.

The father met the son out on the road and did not chide or scold or dole out his punishment.

Grace is when you are given gift on top of gift that you don't deserve. Grace is the ring and the robe. Grace is the feast and the dancing and the party.

Grace is the Father's wholehearted embrace.

Because the Father loves all his children without partiality, He equally offers mercy and grace to both the elder son and the prodigal. In his magnificent book *The Return of the Prodigal*, Henri Nouwen writes, "The joy at the dramatic return of the younger son in no way means that the elder son was less loved, less appreciated, less favored. He loves them both with a complete love and expresses that love according to their individual journeys. He knows them both intimately. He understands their unique gifts and shortcomings. . . . The father responds to both according to their uniqueness. The return of the younger son makes him call for a joyful celebration. The return of the elder son makes him extend an invitation to full participation in that joy."[2]

what about consequences?

We are all equally in need of mercy and grace and the Father's embrace. If you are dealing with a sin issue, you probably already know that all sin is wrong and that it's pointless to try and categorize types of sin or put them on some kind of rating scale. But why do some falls seem so much worse than others? I believe it's because different sins carry different levels of consequences.

Jesus made it clear in his Sermon on the Mount that inner sin is equally as bad as wrong behavior in the eyes of God. However, we all know that someone who acts on the adulterous thoughts in her or his heart is going to experience more painful consequences, and so are others who love and look up to that person.

Someone who thinks about killing someone may be sinning, but no one will know the difference. His consequences are in his own heart. They're between him and God. But the person who carries out murder traumatically impacts the lives (and deaths) of others.

The steps of restoration, such as those I walked through with my church, are going to look different depending on what has happened in your life and who was affected by the consequences. My pastor told me, "Restitution has to be as far and wide as the knowledge of the sin." That's why, for me, it was important for me to go up in front of my church and confess what I'd done and ask forgiveness. The restitution required to make things as right as you humanly can may be a smaller circle for somebody else, or it may be a bigger circle, depending on the circumstances.

taking responsibility

It is vital to accept responsibility in your part of any sort of fall or failure so that you can be healed, so you won't repeat the pattern in your future. When my first husband and I knew that our marriage was headed for divorce, our counselor asked us to come back for one more session and asked both of us to address how we failed the marriage. Not how the other person failed, but how we each, individually, failed the marriage. We had to say, "Here is what I did, here is how I let the marriage down, here is how I've failed."

When you address your part of the responsibility in any failure through confession, apology, or action, it isn't about heaping more guilt on yourself. It's about putting the past behind you. We all are forgiven, but some of us may be able to put our sin behind us a little quicker than others. Restitution is making the wrong you have done as right as you can.

However, let's face it: there are some wrongs that we cannot make right. Once the feathers are out of the pillow, there is no way to get all those feathers back in. We simply have to grieve and accept the all-encompassing mercy and grace of our Father. Then we must ask for the forgiveness of others after we express our sorrow.

For me, restitution meant going to my former husband and going to Don's former wife and asking their forgiveness. It also meant going to our children, our friends, and everyone else we'd lied to. We apologized over and over. It was emotionally draining.

Though God forgave us right away, it took many of the hurting, wounded human beings around us a lot longer to heal. Even after more than a decade, some still cannot forgive. They are all too human, as are we. Sometimes we still struggle with forgiving ourselves. We experience what Don and I call "pop-up" pain—at times our hearts ache with the heaviness of what we did and the fallout that lingers, especially when we see how we hurt our kids.

When "pop-up" pain happens and I feel frozen in my failure, I just try to imagine my Father running down the road to meet me.

I look in his eyes—brimming with acceptance—and remember that it isn't about my failures, it is about His love. It is about being God's beloved daughter, who is always welcome home. Then I dry my tears, lift my eyes toward heaven, and sing with all the gratitude my heart can hold the song He gave back to me.

Whether I am the younger son, or the elder son, God's only desire is to bring me home.

— HENRI NOUWEN

3 falling into soft, safe places

He tends his flock like a shepherd: He gathers the lambs
in his arms and carries them close to his heart.

—ISAIAH 40:11

You may have seen the famous quote by actress Bette Davis: "Old age is no place for sissies." It does seem sadly ironic that when we are at our feeblest, entering our "golden years," we are often called upon to make some of life's most difficult choices.

In a similar way, when you are spiritually faltering, stumbling, or spread-eagle at the bottom of some pit of your life, you are already at your weakest. And yet it is at these times that you need to make some of the wisest and most difficult decisions of your life. Unfair? Well, yes! But then, our mamas told us that life isn't fair, didn't they?

One thing I hope I am able to do in this chapter is to help you gather what I call "The Great Triage" around yourself. These are the bare essentials to help you survive any crisis of soul. I have found that there are three things broken people need in order to fall forward.

31

First, you need people who will be "Jesus with skin on." A few "unshockable" saints who don't try to *see through you* but instead show up in work clothes with their spiritual sleeves rolled up to try to help *see you through*. They are the good Samaritans among us who don't lean back in an above-it-all posture, clicking their tongues, analyzing why you are lying facedown in the dirt. They simply bring bandages and try to get you where help can be found. They are the "safe people." You'll need them in spades. And for a while, perhaps a long while, you'll need to put barriers up to protect yourself from "unsafe people." (More about how to recognize the safe from the unsafe in a bit.)

Second, you need a "safe place", a physical space apart from the madding crowd where you can have the space and time and nurturing environment that will help you to find your life's balance, your sanity, and your faith again.

Third, you need a "safe God." Not, mind you, a tame God. Not a watered-down version of God. But a great and powerful God who is as tender as a Shepherd is with his littlest lost lamb. Your view of God probably needs a bit of realigning. I have discovered that most stumbles and falls are precipitated by a false idea of who God is and the resulting rebellion away from that false image of God we've created in our minds.

safe people

Let's talk first about safe versus unsafe people. Unfortunately, it is not easy to know this ahead of time. If I've heard this story once, I've heard it in a hundred different forms. "When I found myself at the bottom of my life," someone will confess, "when I needed my friends the most, it was an absolute *shock* to discover that the people I thought would be with me forever, no matter what, fled the scene of my pain as quickly as possible." Some of these friends are Christians, and they're well meaning. But for whatever reason, they have a difficult (or impossible) time accepting that you are not the person they *thought* you were. Some are frightened by the pain of the place you find yourself in. Some people just don't know what to do or say, and so they say nothing. And some find their voices and lay on the "Christian" condemnation—as if it's not obvious that you're already lying in the dirt.

There were friends that I truly thought I would be friends with forever, but when I began to make choices that they couldn't support (and I don't blame them), they walked away from our friendship. Honestly, I don't hold it against them. Sometimes we as friends ask far too much of others. I know I did.

But then there will be other more pleasant surprises. Some of your friends will astonish you with their ability to stand beside you no matter how deep the muck becomes. I have three girlfriends (we call ourselves the ya-yas), and we've been friends for more than twenty years. Much has changed in our individual lives since we became friends, but we all made a commitment early on that we would be there for each other, no matter what. That promise has been tested a time or two, but we are still the ya-yas—just a bit older and hopefully wiser.

Other people you hardly know, people who had been on the

fringes of your life, will step into the mess of your life and become heroes to you. These new friends seem to come out of nowhere! I don't know why this happens, but I've heard it enough times to know that it's one of the ways God works in the lives of the hurting. He brings the most unlikely helpers and healers to the scene. Remember the parable of the man who was stripped, beaten, and robbed on the road to Jericho? The priest did not help this man. Nor did the Levite. These two holy men—the ones we'd expect to lend a hand—did not help but instead gave the downed man a wide berth and walked on by. It was the Samaritan, the person who (in those days) was not expected to be a friend, who saved the poor man's life.

There was a woman at my church who had gone through a divorce. For several months, she really reached out to me—she would call me or meet me for coffee. I would ask her, "Did you go through this? What about that?" It was wonderful the way she just allowed me to process without judgment. After a few months, I didn't see her as much. I was beginning to feel a little more confident in my journey. But for that season, she was vital in my life.

I have laughingly said, "If you want to clear your overbooked network of friends, try having a huge crisis in your life." What is left is pure gold. These are the friends who'll be with you on your deathbed. Sure, their number may be small. Yes, you may even be able to count them on one finger, but oh, what a precious gift to truly know who your friends are. It has been said that a true friend is someone who walks in when the rest of the world walks out. I would agree.

I love the saying, "People come into our lives for a reason, a season, or a lifetime." Now that my life is out in the light and I've been cautiously accepted back into the Christian fold, many who were reluctant to embrace me when I was at my lowest are now willing to forgive. I truly appreciate this, and I also understand why they might have wanted, even needed, to separate from me for a time. However, I will never forget the few brave souls who risked their own reputations to cross the street and bring the bandages. These are my safe people. If they stayed with me when the spotlight went dark, I know these friends will be with me until we walk into heaven together.

In Donald McCullough's book *The Wisdom of Pelicans*, he writes about a tribe in South Africa, the Babemba tribe, whose tradition is to surround any person who failed in some way, to remind them of who they really are. "All work ceases, and all the men, women, and children gather in a large circle around the accused. Then each person, one by one, speaks to him about all the good things he has done in his lifetime." This ceremony can last several days, and "once the circle is broken, a joyous celebration takes place, and the person is welcomed back into the tribe."[1]

Can you imagine what would happen if Christians took this sort of position in the face of someone who is facedown in their failure? I had a few people who were my personal "Babembas," such as my parents. I remember finally getting the nerve to tell my parents that I was getting a divorce and that I was in love with someone else. The other end of the phone was very, very quiet for what seemed like an eternity. And then I remember them both saying, "Sandi, we love you. You will always be our daughter, and we will always be here for you."

My church also became a safe place for me. I felt as if I was going to be bombarded with judgment, but instead I found a safe place where God could confront me. I learned that loving and supporting someone in the tough times doesn't mean you agree with the person's wrong choices, it just means that you don't withdraw your love from her or him. These people stood by me. They asked tough questions, but they didn't run.

Thankfully, my safe tribe also reminded me that I was not past redemption or beyond God's forgiveness. I take a lot of comfort in the story of Peter, who denied Jesus three times after knowing him very, very well. When Jesus, in his resurrected form, saw Peter again, He gave him no lectures but instead he showered him with love, affirmation, and a new opportunity to affirm Him—three times. Oh, I can get my arms around a Savior like this!

There's another poignant affirmation of Peter's forgiveness in the Bible that is usually overlooked. After Christ's death and resurrection, the angel at the empty tomb tells the women gathered there to "go, tell his disciples and Peter, 'He is going ahead of you into Galilee. There you will see him, just as he told you'" (Mark 16:7). Now, you and I both know that the angel could have simply included Peter in with the "disciples," but it was as if God Himself, through the angel, wanted Peter to know that personal forgiveness for his betrayal had already been accomplished. Often in Scripture, you see the Lord calling people by name. He sees us not as a big mass of nameless humanity, but as individuals who are deeply known and even more deeply loved. Talk about safety!

safe places

I've never felt as lost and alone as I did during the fallout of my failures. Thankfully, some of my ya-ya friends recommended I get away to a safe place where I could find the inner healing I needed so badly. So, one day I walked into the offices of New Life Clinic.

I'm not sure what I was expecting—maybe a cozy little cabin somewhere—but it turned out to be the psych ward of a hospital. There was nothing comfy and cozy about it! Actually, it was a little eerie. I thought, *Am I crazy? Is that why I'm here?* Then I met my angel, the woman who would become my therapist for the week, Deborah. She met me at the elevator, looked me in the eye, and held out her hand to me. Instead of shaking it, I reached out and hugged her. She said she was so glad I was there and she was proud of me for coming. She assured me that this was a safe place. The funny thing was that, even though it was a psych ward, I felt at home. I was ready to work.

I spent two weeks there, and it was one of the best gifts I've given myself. A place to really "lean into" the emotions and feelings, the hurts and the pain. It was a luxury to not have to stuff it all back down to go home and fix dinner or hurry to a meeting. I could let it all hang out, emotionally, for two weeks.

When I checked out of New Life, I knew I needed to make my home a safe place where my children and I could begin to heal together. A safe place is somewhere you can go and feel completely at ease, completely yourself, completely at rest.

Sometimes we need actual sanctuaries where we can go to cocoon and refuel. Jesus took breaks and often sought out beautiful sacred spaces where he could feel restful and prayerful. It is a lovely idea for anyone at any season of life to create a little "Eden corner" in their home as a place to refocus, relax, reconnect with God, and remember what's really important. However, it is essential for anyone who is hurting, struggling, faltering, or recovering.

If you're able to create such a place, try to bring in elements of color, art, scent, and sound that you find soothing. Taking a paintbrush in hand and tackling a wall with fresh color can be a therapy unto itself. I have a friend, Becky, who was in the throes of grief from a divorce. On Mother's Day that year, her adult children showed up at the front door with buckets of soft, lemony yellow paint and spent the day transforming her kitchen and living room with liquid sunshine. She remembers, "The next few mornings when I woke up, I would still cry a little, but I found it hard to stay down for long in those happy rooms."

When her husband left, another of my friends turned her bedroom back into a replica of the one she'd loved as a teenager, simply to try to reconnect with who she was before she was a wife. Another, desperate for laughter in a dark time, redecorated her bathroom in bright, childlike comic strip characters.

I have converted the top of my dresser into my prayer altar, my little "Eden spot." I have candles, a prayer box where I put prayer requests and answers, and my favorite inspirational books. Just looking at this peaceful place calms my heart. It symbolizes, for me, my peace in the midst of the storm.

Of course, there are other ways to find a safe place to heal. You may find that what works for you doesn't fit your preconceived notion of a place of rest, such as a spa or the home of a dear friend. For one of my friends, a safe place meant somewhere she could escape from the difficult realities of her own life for a few hours a day—so she took a job as a Starbucks barista for a year.

She says, "I was lonely and depressed, and my marriage was struggling. Some of my friends were finding it difficult to support me in this time of crisis. I needed a social outlet, and I needed an environment where I could work hard and be focused on something other than *my life* for a while. As it turned out, I loved serving others, and I loved how the job kept me in the mind-set of being a servant while keeping my mind occupied. Eventually Starbucks became a crucial facet of my healing process, allowing me brief respites from my troubles so that I could come back to my family refreshed and ready to make it work. Our marriage has gone through an incredible healing process, and my life is so much better now. Starbucks was a safe place to heal and gain strength for an incredible, growth-filled year. Being a barista was truly a gift to me."

healthy view of God

Even though you may have been taught as a child that God is good and God is love, you may have a hard time grasping the truth of this when it comes to yourself personally. If your view of God is a condemning one (or even partially this way), I recommend that you immerse yourself in everything the Scriptures say about the love, mercy, grace, and forgiveness of God. Spend as long as it takes dwelling on these Scriptures until you recognize that you are God's beloved daughter and that there is nothing you could do that could make Him love you any more than He does right now. There is nothing you could do that would cause Him to love you any less.

Once you have given yourself this triage of hope—(1) surrounding yourself with safe people; (2) carving out a safe space; (3) soaking up the truth of God's love and revising your view of God—you are well on your way to falling forward. You cannot possibly fall into the arms of a God you don't trust. For many of us, this is the most important turning point of all. If you hesitate to fall into the arms of God, there's a good chance you don't yet know the depth, the height, or the breadth of His deep, deep love for you.

There's no time like today to fall in love with the One who waits to catch you up in His strong, gentle arms.

I began to wonder if becoming a Christian did not work more like falling in love than agreeing to a list of true principles.

— DONALD MILLER, AUTHOR OF *BLUE LIKE JAZZ*

Survival Tips
(extra help for the early days following a crisis)

1. You might feel like you are losing your memory or going crazy. Don't worry—this is normal. Just go with it!

2. Keep your tasks for each day small and short. Make lists. This will clear your mind just a bit and unburden your over-taxed brain. Write each one down and check them off—even if your list says, "Get up. Get dressed. Cry. Dry tears. Eat. Nap. Cry. Get undressed. Pray for the day to end. Sleep."

3. Have a good cry if you need to, whenever you can. Tears are a language God understands, and they clear your body of built-up toxins.

4. Laugh as soon as you possibly can, even if it is dark humor. You'll know you will live through this the minute you can laugh. One of my favorite lines from the movie *Steel Magnolias* is when Dolly Parton's character says, "Laughter through tears is my favorite emotion."

5. You may feel like you need to be demoted to life's slow class. You probably won't be able to read a lot, and the Bible may seem daunting. Be gentle with yourself. Meditate on one or two comforting Scriptures or quotes. Talk to God as if He were your friend, and tell Him everything without fear. He can take it.

6   Remind yourself that if you've survived thus far, you'll make it around the bend and be stronger than ever before. You are probably already starting to grasp one of the gifts of having been in crisis. You get the gift of perspective—it is very clear now what matters and what doesn't.

7   Visualize yourself in the arms of Jesus. Let Him hold you and remind you that you are His beloved child. Your picture is still on His refrigerator.

8   Breathe in, breathe out, put one foot in front of the other. Some of these early days are simply about endurance, holding on, and letting time do its work. You will feel better. You will survive.

9   Hold your loved ones close, especially if they are able to express their love in kind and helpful ways.

10 If none of the above works for you, you might do what I did—go to a batting cage! I would spend about fifteen minutes trying to hit the stuffing out of a baseball. Every time I would swing, I would really get into it, sometimes even imagining that I was hitting the problems right out of my life. It worked for me!

4 falling into joyful choices

I have set before you life and death, blessings and curses.
Now choose life, so that you and your children may live.

— DEUTERONOMY 30:19

At Women of Faith events this past year, my friend Patsy master-
fully unraveled some beautiful treasures from John 5, where Jesus
met the man lying by the pool called Bethesda, waiting for the angel
to "trouble the waters" so that he could be healed. Apparently, this
man had been chronically ill for thirty-eight years. We don't know
what his ailment was exactly, but we can be pretty sure it was more
serious than a head cold. Knowing how long the man had been living the life of a disabled beggar, Jesus asked him a startling question: "Do you want to get well?" Or, in other words, "Are you
earnest about doing what it takes to get healing?"

Talk about a ridiculous question. Duh! The poor man had been
lounging around the pool for decades just waiting and hoping for
his turn in the tub o' healing waters. Of course, the guy wanted to
get well! Right?

Right?

Well, maybe. This invalid lay by the pool, day after day, year after year and, tragically, somehow always missed his chance for healing. There was never anyone available to help him, he said. Someone else always beat him to the water's edge. It seems a forgone conclusion that he'd desperately want to get well.

But Jesus knows the true thoughts and intentions of our hearts, and so maybe he knew something humans could not see. Maybe this guy was getting some hidden perks by postponing his healing. Maybe he had come to depend on the pity he got for always being the last one to the pool. Perhaps he was afraid of getting well and having to get a job doing something besides shaking a cup. Jesus always had an uncanny bead on unseen truth: not everyone really wants to get well, and certainly not everyone is willing to pay the price for emotional healing.

In her book *Beauty for Ashes*, Joyce Meyer (herself the victim of many years of abuse) wrote about the beggar at Bethesda: "This man, like so many people today, had a deep-seated and lingering disorder for a long, long time. After thirty-eight years, he had learned, I am sure, how to function with his disorder. People who are in prison function, but they are not free. However, sometimes prisoners—whether physical or emotional—become so accustomed to being in bondage that they settle in with their condition and learn to live with it."[1]

I wonder how many of us have been kidnapped and are held in emotional bondage to fear, abuse memories, guilt, unforgiveness, rage, sorrow, regrets, or the belief that we are somehow unloved or unwanted or defected. Living like this keeps you locked away from real life. It keeps you at arm's length from intimacy and the abundant life of which Jesus spoke.

Sometimes we have to honestly ask ourselves, "Am I getting any benefit from staying sick and holding on to my role as victim or loser?" I found it was tempting to stay mentally stuck on one sad page of my life and never fall forward into freedom. I could easily dismiss all the wonderful chapters that came before the one titled "The Year from Hell When 'Good Sandi' Fell"— and never allow the Author of my life to write new stories and chapters that glow with God's mercy and grace and renewal.

In what ways could labeling ourselves as "Losers" with permanent markers be giving us some subtle emotional perks?

If I'm brazenly honest, I can think of a few side benefits of staying the emotionally/spiritually weak sister or brother. For one thing, if you are a loser, no one expects much of you. If you stay bent low with an enormous burden of pain, resentment, or guilt on your back, you are less of a target to Christians who might want to put you down in order to feel better about themselves. If you actually accept God's forgiveness and forgive others—if you let the Great Physician heal you from the inside out and you emerge whole and healthy and well—you'll have to get out of your sickbed and give it to someone who needs it more than you do. Doggone it, you might actually have to make yourself useful in God's kingdom again!

In addition, you may have to find a way to gently turn away the irritation of those who were more comfortable when you were the alcoholic, or the unstable sibling or the daughter who couldn't get her act together. Sadly, there are usually at least a few family members or friends who will think you are too big for your britches if you decide to grow up and take custody of your own life and move on toward freedom and joy and service to others. They may have their own dysfunctional baggage and don't really want you to leave the small box of your former identity and begin living larger, happier, freer. They may subconsciously feel threatened when you try to exit your assigned role. Maybe they needed someone in their lives who was doing worse than they were so they could feel superior. What does it matter?

Consider for a moment: if you are a beautiful, free, and beloved child of God, does your continuing to play the victim best serve the world? T. D. Jakes makes the insightful point that our ministry usually comes from the misery we've survived. Some of us have lingered too long in our sickbeds and need to get up out of them because there are others who need the bed you were in. And they need you to tend to their broken hearts with the empathy perhaps only you can give.[2]

I urge you to consider making a choice, right now, today, to get well. Even if all you can pray right now is, "God, help me be willing to be *willing*"—it's a beginning, that important first step.

One of the songs we're working on for my next CD is called "Step into Joy," and it's about deciding whether you are going to stay on the sidelines and whine, "Why doesn't joy ever come to me?" or step right into it. I love the story in Joshua 3 where God instructed the Israelites to cross the river Jordan. That river was roaring! But God promised he'd make a way. Verses 15–16 say,

"Now the Jordan is at flood stage all during harvest. Yet as soon as the priests who carried the ark reached the Jordan and their feet touched the water's edge, the water from upstream stopped flowing." Did you catch that? They actually had to step into the river *before* God parted the waters. God blesses our baby steps of faith.

If you've ever had a garden of any kind, you know that God is the One who does the miracle in making the seed grow. However, you also know that you had to get out of your bed, plant the seed, water it, and weed it. Growing fruits, veggies, or flowers is a partnership between the gardener and the Creator.

The same is true for getting well. It has to be a partnership between you and God. God will bless, guide, lead, and heal. But you have to seek out the help. You have to dial the number of a recommended counselor. You have to read books that will help retrain your brain. You have to have a "come to Jesus" moment every day, then put the pedal to the metal to proactively seek out the help you need. When the man at the pool of Bethesda assured Jesus he wanted to get well, Jesus said, "Get up! Pick up your mat and walk" (John 5:8). He asked the man to *do something* to prove his desire was sincere.

I'm going to be really vulnerable with you right now. I was telling my buddy Steve Arterburn about how I really wanted to lose weight. Steve is the host of the national *New Life Live* radio show and writes excellent books on emotional and spiritual healing. However, I've learned that as charming as Steve can be, he tends to call a spade a spade. When I told him my desire, he replied, "Oh really? Well if you really want this with all your heart, then you've got to commit to doing twenty minutes of exercise a day, four days a week."

Oh. Well. *Hmmmm.*

I had to think to myself, *How badly do I really want to lose weight? Am I willing to take the necessary steps toward that professed desired goal?* If not, then you know what? I'm not quite ready to get well in this area. (See the end of this chapter for an update on this story!)

So you see, I'm not preaching to you about making a choice to get well because I've got it down pat in all areas of my life. I still have areas in which I want to grow, and I need friends who will hold my feet to the fire to make it happen. It's tough to have friends who call you on your stuff, your excuses, your whining. But if they love you, they'll tell you the truth.

What I have learned is that lasting change means to conscientiously make three joyful choices: the choice *to reveal,* the choice *to heal,* and the choice *to be real.* (And isn't it just too cute how they all rhyme?)

the choice to reveal

The first thing we have to do in order to begin reclaiming joy is to be willing to be vulnerable—an open book, warts and all, before God and at least one other person (a counselor or trusted friend). There's another story in the Bible about a woman falling forward, in the right direction, toward Jesus. She had some kind of disease that involved bleeding, and for twelve years she had consulted every healer imaginable. No one had been able to help her. Just imagine how desperate she must have been! When she heard Jesus was coming to town, she must have known He was her last hope. But He was surrounded by crowds, and in the crush of people, she could not get His attention. She barely managed to simply touch the edge of His garment—and she was healed! Not only that, but Jesus stopped in His tracks, having felt some power go out of Him, and asked that whoever had touched Him would *reveal* herself or himself.

Luke 8:47 says, "Then the woman, seeing that she could not go unnoticed, came trembling and fell at his feet. In the presence of all the people, she told why she had touched him and how she had been instantly healed." I love that phrase, "the woman saw that *she could not go unnoticed*." Jesus sees and notices every little thing about us. Jesus saw her and felt compassion for her, and the power went out of Him to cure her. The woman was rewarded by her choice to *reveal herself*, and Jesus told her, "Your faith has healed you" (verse 48).

All that stuff we think we are hiding is actually an open book before His compassionate eyes anyway. So you may as well just relax, open up, and let the Healer do His job and start the process of setting you free. Allow the Great Physician to do any surgery He needs to do to remove old infested wounds that are holding you back.

So many women are walking around with tumors of secrets, cancerous emotions, or broken spirits that have mended the wrong way because they weren't tended to in a healthy way. The first step in falling forward is to reveal your deepest hurts and struggles to God and then to one other safe person.

the choice to heal

What is the difference between those who become more alive and beautiful and get *better* after crisis or loss and those who grow old, ugly, and *bitter?* I think those who get better have learned the secret of gleaning the lessons from their losses. They do not waste their pain.

Those who grow bitter seem to have an especially hard time openly asking God to teach them something of eternity, particularly after they either have experienced a major loss or have fouled up in some way. They may no longer trust God because He didn't protect them from their pain. They might even be afraid that God will point His finger at them, saying they don't deserve His help, that they are not worthy of healing. So they deflect and reject and play the blame game and never allow God to enter into the most secret part of their hearts and lovingly heal what is wrong and forgive what has been done.

People who get better, on the other hand, allow God into the center of their situations, *expecting* healing. They ask God not only to walk with them through the pain, but to redeem their sorrow so that their future can be better.

The Bible is full of examples of people who gleaned understanding from their pain as well as people who stubbornly refused to heed the lessons leading to emotional and spiritual health. I think of the Israelites who spent forty years wandering in the wilderness, around and around in circles. Why? They didn't grasp the lessons of Gratitude 101. They were the ultimate glass-half-empty group of gripers. They grumbled and whined their way through the wilderness, blind to all of God's blessings and provisions.

On the other hand, there was Paul who "caught" the lessons of gratitude, particularly in his letter to the Philippians. He asked God to help him see his bleak circumstances with an attitude of thankfulness, and soon the very chains that held him bound in prison became something to be grateful for. "*Because of my chains*, most of the brothers in the Lord have been encouraged to speak the word of God more courageously and fearlessly" (Philippians 1:14, emphasis added).

At this season of Paul's life, he had learned the lessons of a grateful spirit so well that the book is overflowing with the word *joy*—despite his circumstances being less than ideal, to say the least. (Most of us would consider being chained to a Roman guard 24/7 to be something of an inconvenience.) Paul shares at the end of the book that he has learned the secret of contentment so that he can live just as happily in riches or in poverty, in prison or free—and in fact, he actually spends a bit of time discussing whether it would be better to live or to die. Now that's a free man! He saw that all circumstances carry with them some lessons that lift us closer to God if we allow the Lord to use them for our good.

the choice to become real

One of the most beloved children's books of all time has to be *The Velveteen Rabbit*. If you've not read it, you must. It is the charming allegorical tale of a little stuffed rabbit who lands in a nursery where some of the toys have become "real" over time. The toy rabbit wants nothing more than to learn the secret of how to become real, so he turns to the wise old Skin Horse, who has become real himself. This sets up one of the most poignant conversations in the book, beginning with the Velveteen Rabbit asking, "What is Real?"

"Real isn't how you are made," replies the Skin Horse. "It's a thing that happens to you. When a child loves you for a long, long time, not just to play with, but REALLY loves you, then you become Real."

"Does it hurt?" asked the Rabbit.

"Sometimes," said the Skin Horse, for he was always truthful. "When you are Real you don't mind being hurt."

"Does it happen all at once, like being wound up," he asked, "or bit by bit?"

"It doesn't happen all at once," said the Skin Horse. "You become. It takes a long time. That's why it doesn't happen often to people who break easily, or have sharp edges, or who have to be carefully kept. Generally, by the time you are Real, most of your hair has been loved off, and your eyes drop out and you get loose in your joints and very shabby. But these things don't matter at all, because once you are Real you can't be ugly, except to people who don't understand."[3]

How do Christians become real? Well, we become real when God "loves you for a long, long time." And we become real when we realize that He doesn't love us just so He can "play with us"— mess with our heads and emotions—but "real happens" the day you realize He *really* loves you, down to the depths of your being.

Now the hard question. "Does it hurt?"

Well, yes, it does sometimes. By the time you've been through the process of becoming real, you feel a lot like the Velveteen Rabbit looks at the end of the story: shabbier and looser in the joints; your eyes may even be drooping. But here is one of life's great paradoxes: your "image" no longer seems to matter as much because you are happy to be loved so deeply, to finally be real.

In Luke 22:7–60, there's a long story about Simon Peter's journey from being a brand-new disciple—full of vigor and self-assurance—through the valley of disappointing himself and the One he loves most. But through this realization of his fallenness and a deeper understanding of the love and mercy of His best friend, Jesus, Peter emerges shabbier but more beautifully real. Before Peter's denial of Christ, right before the crucifixion, Jesus warned him that the enemy "has asked to sift you as wheat" (v. 31). He also assured Peter that He had already been praying for him. I can't help but think of "sifting" as being a lot like the often painful process that the Velveteen Rabbit had to endure to become real. What does sifting mean? In biblical days, it meant the wheat was put through a sieve to separate the grain from the chaff. Beth Moore writes, "Christ . . . permits us to be sifted to shake out the real from the unreal, the trash from the true."[4]

In Peter's case, what was sifted out of him? Moore observes that the enemy "observed Peter's overconfidence and propensity toward pride. He surmised that when the sifting came, every page would come up chaff. He was wrong. Christ knew Peter's heart. He knew that underneath Peter's puffed-up exterior was a man with a genuine heart for God. Jesus knew that Peter could deny Christ to others, but he could not deny Christ to himself. He would be back—a revised edition with a new jacket."⁵

The best leaders are those who realize that they are totally dependent on God to do their job. Often they don't even aspire to lead, but others notice qualities of empathy, integrity, trust, and a realness of heart, and they simply end up in leadership positions because others trust them. The people who are the best Christ-followers I know have had some of their fur rubbed off. They've been sifted and humbled and are now more compassionate, more genuine and authentic in their lives and loves.

A new friend of mine told me how she went through a time of losing her stellar Christian reputation a few years ago after some poor choices. But in her valley of pain, she chose to reveal her heart to safe people who helped her with her choice to heal. And now she's surprised by how the extra weight of pride and perfectionism was sifted out of her and how wonderful it feels to be able to be the same person on the inside that she is on the outside. She said, "Sandi, I was recently at a dinner with lots of 'important' Christian leaders, people I might have desperately wanted to impress a few years ago. Most of them knew of my mistakes. You might have thought I'd have felt uncomfortable or self-conscious. But just the opposite was true. I felt this surprising but glorious lightness in my spirit. A gratefulness for not having to waste energy polishing my so-called 'perfect image' or feeling compelled to come across as a woman who had it all together. In fact, it was freeing just to be who I was and focus on truly caring for others at the table. Maybe it is because I have a new compassion for how many Christian leaders are working so hard to keep up their perfect images. I just want to reach out and say, 'You can be your true self with me, and with God, and we'll both love you to pieces.'"

I could identify with my friend's experience. Oh, the freedom that comes from following the choices to reveal, to heal, and to allow yourself to become real. It reminds me of a quote I read from Margaret Mitchell, the Southern belle who penned *Gone with the Wind*: "Until you've lost your reputation, you never realize what a burden it was or what freedom really is."[6]

One day I sat down and wrote out my thoughts about my own vulnerable time of sifting and healing and allowing God to see all the things I thought I'd hidden so well. I'll close this chapter with this poem as my velveteen gift, from one love-worn bunny to another.

LAYERS

A word about this song. These lyrics are probably the most vulnerable I have ever been about the issue of my weight. As I began to understand the underlying reasons for not shedding pounds, these lyrics began to flow out of my soul.

Buried deep beneath this skin lies a child full of hope
Let her out, let her soar
Why do you cover her with your shame, why do you layer her
with your guilt?

falling *for*ward

Tell her she's been set free, tell her she's okay

Tell her she doesn't have to be ashamed and hide behind the
  armor

Of false protection and guilt

She trusts in the lie that says she will never be safe

And that she will never know freedom and love and peace

But you can tell her, you can give her wings

You can help her speak

She shies as she listens—she can't believe it's true

No more hiding, no more layers of the lies that cage her in

She's a beauty, she's a princess

She's a woman-child with much to say

Just knowing, she stands taller, she stands prouder

She stands sure

All she needed was permission to lose the cravings of her shame

It was she who held on tight and not the chains that bound

I can see her in the distance, running, arms open wide

Longing to be known, longing to be loved, longing to belong

Craving union with her soul, craving fullness of contentment

And I hold her in my heart and I welcome my old friend

It is this that leaves her full

Coming home to all of me, more of me, less of me

And the layers of protection begin to melt away on sight

No longer needed as a buffer

She walks naked into the light, exposing all of her to His mercy
  and His love

Not holding back, she dances into my arms of love

Lyrics by Sandi Patty 2006

56

In the time since I first wrote this chapter, I have some good "waist management" progress to report. I felt that God was asking me to walk every week for about 120 minutes—but most important, to concentrate on enjoying the journey: the beauty around me, the time away from my harried life. If I reach that goal and enjoy the experience, I consider myself "sober" for that week.

Here's the good news: I am blessed to say that I have been "sober" now for ten weeks.

Enjoy the journey. The blessings will find you along the falling forward way!

5 falling into a whole new you

How precious to me are your thoughts, O God! How vast is the sum of them!

— PSALM 139:17

I always thought it was hard to transition from singing for the president to comforting a kid with the stomach virus. I used to tell my road people that what we do is *real* but it is not the *real world*. The real world is homework and dance lessons, basketball practice and church youth groups. It's holding your kid's head over the commode so they won't hurt themselves when they are throwing up in the middle of the night. No housekeeper from the hotel to clean that up!

When my babies would wake up in the middle of the night with the beginnings of an ear infection, it didn't matter to them that I may have just arrived home at 2:00 a.m. on the bus after singing for thousands. They needed their mom. I used to feel that I had to take this "on stage persona" and try to somehow translate that super image into my "off stage" everyday life. Turns out, exactly opposite is true.

Because although the lyrics to the songs I sing are are real and true, the life of fame, if you will, is not reality. Someone said, "Never read your press. You are never as bad as they say or as good as they say." It's easy to get tangled up in "What does everyone think about me?" and then try hard to portray the right image. And then, eventually, most of us fall very hard off of that self-imposed pedestal at some point in our lives.

Gloria Gaither wrote a beautiful lyric that began one night after I had been on stage with the Gaither Trio. (I used to travel and sing with them earlier in my career.) We were changing clothes and getting our bags out to the bus to head to yet another show in another town on yet another night. We had to walk across the now vacant stage to get to the loading dock. It was pretty stark except for one work light in the middle of the stage.

Bill looked at the stage and said, "The stage is bare, the crowds are gone." And thus began the seed of the lyrics for "The Stage Is Bare." My favorite line in that song is "Don't miss the eternity in the daily days"—a reminder to marvel in what the world often sees as mundane. The song also speaks of who we are when the spotlight dims, and we are without the makeup, the script, the backup band, and an adoring audience.

Though you may never have known the odd transition from being a stage performer to being your kids' mom or experienced walking onto an empty stage once the curtain has come down, my guess is that you know what it's like to have the lights dimmed on the life you knew before your crisis, and you wonder who you are now that the trappings of who you once were have been altered in some way. Without your makeup or your "I'm just fine" script, without the role you once played without effort, who are you?

Most of us who've gone through a significant crisis or failure find ourselves in transition to a "new normal." The newly divorced or widowed ask, "Who am I without my husband now?" Someone who loses her job may ask, "Who am I apart from what I do?" With the last child off to college, some moms ask, "Who am I without children to care for? And who is this man I'm married to?"

When relationships are permanently altered in painful ways, almost always a real crisis of identity is attached. One grieving woman shared, "Our marriage coming apart was agonizing—like a muscle being torn away from its shell in slow, torturous increments. It seemed my identity was so wrapped up in our couplehood that I was truly lost in ways I hadn't expected without the other half of my heart."

When a couple comes apart after many years or someone loses a close loved one (either by death or separation), a psychic injury, an excruciatingly painful tear to the mind and emotion is created. (Even the partner who leaves a marriage and expresses the desire to divorce is often ambushed with sadness, sorrow, and regrets he or she had not anticipated.) Any upset or loss between two people who were once as close as "peas and carrots"—to borrow Forrest Gump's description—can leave a psychological rip in your heart that leaves you feeling unmoored for a long time. Even long-time friendships between women that come unraveled can be devastatingly disorienting.

who am I *now*?

In her book *The Year of Magical Thinking*, Joan Didion writes of the common grief phenomena of expecting the one who died to come waltzing in the door at any moment. She expected to feel crazed with sorrow after her husband died, but to actually feel like she'd flown over the cuckoo's nest at times came as quite a shock to her once well-ordered mind.[1] Our logic says one thing is true, but it takes *time* for all of our emotions and brain patterns to shift from who we *were* to who we *are*. In fact, there's nearly always a transition time after loss—when you feel suspended, between two trapezes: you before the crisis and you following the crisis.

Some of us experience multiple losses at once, which simply magnify our sense of "Who am I?" One woman said:

My husband's midlife crisis and sudden, shocking exit from our marriage occurred just as my nest of children was also being emptied. Then I made an unwise decision to move to a secluded, quiet community of elderly people, thinking I'd need quiet, peaceful surroundings in which to heal. Wrong! The quiet was deafening. I'd never understood the agony of loneliness until that time. Like most busy wives and mothers, I'd often daydreamed of a room of my own in which I could be creatively contemplative—and alone!

Little did I know the vast difference between lovely solitude and languishing loneliness. I lost so many anchors at once—my husband, my role as full-time mother, my home, and my familiar neighborhood. There were other losses: two deaths and one near-death of close friends or family members in one year. I had no idea who I was anymore. I'd married at seventeen, moving straight from teeny-bopper bedroom to my husband's bed. I had never formed a complete adult identity of my own apart from being a wife and mom.

There was a time I would have declared myself to be the least likely woman to yield to sexual temptation. My own husband had just left me for a younger woman, and I sincerely thought myself incapable of any sort of illicit affair. I knew the pain of it all too well. But now as I look back on the fragile state I was in, I'm not terribly surprised that I fell so hard in the wrong direction. I was so vulnerable, literally starving for connection, for touch, for love! My skin was physically craving tender human touch. I think the loss of being touched may be the loss that hurt the most after our separation. So there I was, adrift in a deep sea of multiple wounds, and before long I fell in love and into sin with a married man, and our affair eventually became public. Both of us were respected Christians with decades of honorable service for God behind us. Now there was pain on top of pain, loss on top of loss, heartache compounded. It took all I could do to keep my head out of the oven in those months when we separated from each other to try to find deeper healing for our aching hearts.

When I asked her to describe the feelings that went with the unraveling of life as she knew it, she said, "Sandi, the best way I can describe what it felt like is that my life picture blew up a bit more with each life 'explosion'—and there were hundreds of little pieces of me, now disconnected and lost, floating here and there. Now and again, I'd catch a glimpse of myself floating by—and then I'd have to choose whether or not to keep that part of the 'me' I once was. It took me several years to connect the old pieces of 'me' with new pieces of the self I was becoming until I'd assembled the jigsaw puzzle of the me I am today—a me and a life I'm so happy with again! Probably happier than I've ever been. But it took time, therapy, dear family, and Velcro friends who stuck with me, along with God's forgiveness, love, and acceptance to get from there to here. They'd remind me of the person I still was to God and to them, with or without a man in my life."

At times of transition following pain, most women who've survived such times and thrived will tell you that it is really important to grasp hold of your true identity. Even if your world and your emotions are crumbling around you, even if you feel as though you've lost your original self through sorrow or mistakes or both, even if others try to pigeonhole you or do armchair analysis, you have to grasp hold of the truth as if it were the only floating log in a stormy sea. Before we look at who you *are*, let's take a brief peek at who you *are not*.

who you are is not the sum
of the wrong you've done

First of all, you are not the sum of your failures. You are not your slips or sins. God doesn't read one page in your life and call it a book. If he did, there would not be an Old Testament "saint" whose life would be honored in the New Testament. And yet when we read the long Faith Hall of Fame list in Hebrews 11, there's not a person among them who didn't blow it, big-time, at one time or another. If God didn't cast our sins into the sea of forgetfulness but instead chose to remember our worst times, this chapter could read very differently. Instead of a list of all the glorious things these saints of old accomplished "by faith," there could be a list of the things they messed up "by sheer human stupidity." Instead of being remembered for building an ark and saving his family, Noah could have been remembered for the time he got naked and drunk and passed out in the tent, embarrassing his family.

Father Abraham could have been called a coward for lying to the king about Sarah being his wife in order to save his own skin—even though it put his wife at risk of being raped.

Moses could have been remembered for his fear of public speaking or his untamed temper.

I could go on and on in this vein because I've read all of their stories. But our gracious God could not. Why? His nature is so kind, His forgiveness so wide—He no longer allows His mind to think for even a second about sin that He has already forgiven. It's gone.

the scarlet women of the Bible

This is, in part, why I believe God takes us where we are. Is He okay with the bad decisions we made? I don't think so. But He uses everything for good. He will always start us moving forward again from the moment we fall at His feet and say, "God, I have really screwed up here." We see that in the story of David and Bathsheba.

Yes, they lost their first baby, but eventually the great King Solomon came from the union of David and Bathsheba. And even further down the lineage came Christ Himself!

In fact, each of the women listed in the book of Matthew in the genealogy of Jesus could probably be nominated as least likely to show up in the Messiah's royal line. Five out of five women listed came with *issues*. Rahab was a prostitute. Tamar seduced her father-in-law. Bathsheba committed adultery. Ruth was a Gentile, considered a pagan and an outsider. Then there was Mary, who was just a young, common peasant girl. A nobody. Just another pregnant teenager. (Though pregnant unwed teens were probably not all that common back then, since stoning was a legitimate punishment and, I'm guessing, quite the effective deterrent.)

Here you have this genealogy that is, typical of the culture, very male driven. Rarely were women ever mentioned in lineages. Yet God seemed to have made a special place in His heart for the Unlikely Five. I wonder if each woman represents, perhaps, the things that generally hold women back from being used greatly of God. In this list we have sexual sins (many of them probably stemming from early sexual abuse); we have someone who feels like a newcomer or outsider to Christianity; and we have a gal who comes from humble means and probably considers herself much too young and insignificant to become anything special. The important point here is that none of these women was remembered for her sins or perceived flaws by New Testament writers. The writers of the Gospels and Letters only remembered these women for the goodness God birthed through them during their time on earth.

I love that! God uses broken men and women. And not just men and women in the Bible.

modern-day saints fall down too

Do you ever think that the great classical or modern-day saints you hear about or read about in books somehow lived above the rest of us peons? I confess I sure do. So it was comforting for me to learn that in a particularly vulnerable chapter in his book *Lectures to My Students*, the great theologian Charles Spurgeon wrote a chapter he called "Minister's Fainting Fits." In it, Spurgeon admitted he had several bouts of great depression in his own life, and that he was prone to a "fainting fit" sort of personality. Interestingly, he cites that these bouts of falling into despondency often happened to him before great successes.

Spurgeon wrote:

Fits of depression come over most of us. Usually, cheerful as we may be, we must at intervals be cast down. The strong are not always vigorous, the wise are not always ready, the brave are not always courageous, and the joyous not always happy. There may be, here and there, men of iron—but surely the rust frets even these. Surely the rust erodes even the most iron of men.[2]

I know this may sound like radical concept to some of you, but the more I've soaked myself in the truth of God's Word, the more I believe who you really *are* isn't always what you *do*. With a nod to Mr. Spurgeon, the strong aren't always ready to arm wrestle a bear; the joyous don't always feel like singing "Zippity-Doo-Dah"; the budget-wise can get crazy at a really good shoe sale; and the purest saint can be thrown off her strong resolve at a low point by a charming guy who seems to peer into the depths of her soul.

you aren't who other people say you are

Though it is true that hurting people hurt people, knowing this doesn't necessarily erase the sting of getting wounded by someone who is stuck in his or her own painful story. It just gives you a bit of perspective.

A friend tells this story: "I was finally learning how to stand up for who I really was in a longtime verbally abusive relationship. One Saturday evening my husband came home and began his usual demeaning of me. I had learned from my Bible study and from a wise counselor not to engage him in conversation when he started in with verbal bashing. I learned not to let the words sink in and not to retaliate either, but to come up with a response that would protect my heart without tearing my husband down. So I calmly asked him to leave so that I could sit down and spend some time with God and remember who I really was in His eyes. Because I was so calm and my voice was steady, my husband had no idea what to do or say. He left, and I opened my Bible and read all the verses I'd marked about how much the Father loves His children. I sat and prayed and asked God to help me remember my true identity—beloved daughter of the King.

"The next morning I went to church alone. During the praise and worship period, a young man who'd been sitting with his wife and kids came up to me and said, 'I know this is going to sound weird, but I was sitting over there praying and I felt strongly that God wanted me to tell you something. Now please don't think I'm crazy, because I've never done this sort of thing, but the impression won't leave.'"

So my friend nodded, silently inviting the young man to continue. He said, "I just feel like God wants me to tell you that you are His beautiful and beloved child. And for you to remember this *is who you really are.*"

My friend related, "There was no way this man could have known that I'd told my husband such similar words the night before, when I said, 'I need to remember who I really am.' So when this man ended his sentence with 'this is who you really are,' I felt as though God Himself had come down and wrapped me up in His arms."

who you *are* is who God says you are

Sometimes when we are in the most pain, God has the kindest and most amazingly brilliant methods of affirming who we are to Him. Though this story is in my other books, it is just too precious not to share here in this chapter. For this is a story of how God tenderly and very personally showed me my true, new identity in *His eyes* barely six months after my marriage to Don.

Don and I had playfully toyed with the idea of adopting a child, thinking it would be nice to have a child our blended family could call "ours"—a child who started out his or her life with us as we now were. We even laughingly thought we'd name the baby "Sam" if it turned out to be a boy. But we never pursued the idea in any serious way.

Little did we know that God, however, took our "what if" musings quite seriously. Out of the blue, a call came in. There was a baby who needed a home, now appearing at a hospital near us. I told Don that if this baby was meant for us, we needed God to whack us on the head in some way so that we'd know with absolute certainty that this baby was meant for us at this time.

We went to the hospital, and the baby boy was beautiful, but still we had questions of whether this was a God thing or just a really crazy idea. Then came the whack on the head. The nurses had given the dark-eyed baby a temporary name and had even written it on the end of his crib. *Sam.* His name was Sam. If that doesn't give you goosebumps, I don't know what will. So we took him home, and all of us, including the kids, adopted him as "ours." It would take me another book to describe the joy he has brought to our home.

I suppose the one thing that never ceases to amaze me is that God entrusted us—*us*—with this vulnerable new life. I'd come to the point of saying, "Okay, God, I know You have forgiven me, and I know You have forgiven Don." But there was something profound about Don and I being handed a baby boy to raise as a couple together. It must have been akin to what David and Bathsheba felt when God gave them baby Solomon. We felt not only God's forgiveness of us as individuals, but His blessing on us as a married couple.

Sam was more than the Father's gracious embrace. Sam was the ring and the robe and the feasting and the dancing. When Don and I get mired in our past failures and caught up in the "Oh, woe is me, what have we done?" routine, all we have to do is look in Sam's eyes and drink from those deep, dark, beautiful pools. What we see reflected there is God's affirmation to us. "See how much I love you? I love you enough and trust you enough to give you the most precious gift to be had on this earth."

Look around you for the blessings God is showering upon you as He affirms His love for you today.

taking the first steps toward the new you

One grieving mother, Melissa, took some time to listen to her heart following the accidental drowning death of her nineteen-year-old son, Joshua. He had the soul of an artist, and to honor him, Melissa had one of his drawings tattooed on her ankle! This middle-aged conservative mother smiles every time she glances at the uniquely designed cross, knowing this is something that Josh never would have expected her to do but would have been delighted about! Then, after listening to her heart and recognizing the scenarios that would help her smile again, Melissa decided to return to college and finish her degree in education. Her ultimate dream is to create a school for children who are more artistically inclined than academically gifted—and help them succeed at learning by using creative, artistic teaching methods.

It is amazing what women can do once they are free from the

chains of regret or guilt, know their true identity in Christ, and learn the fine art of listening to their hearts. If you are struggling with who you are now and where to go next, you might consider securing the help of a Christian life coach. (See references at the back of this book.)

One of the most courageous examples of a freed-up woman in my life is my friend Patsy Clairmont. Every week as I watch her take the stage at Women of Faith, I am astounded at the work God has done in her. She will freely share with anyone that she was an agoraphobic—which means she was housebound in her self-imposed prison of fear. She hated being around people and being in large crowds. She shares with all of us that as she began to pray and ask God for healing, He gently said to her, "Patsy, just get up and make the bed." And she would respond, "But God, that is so small. I want to do great things for you!" And He would respond to her spirit by saying, "Get up and make the bed."

To think that Patsy was ever so emotionally paralyzed that just making the bed was her big accomplishment of the day astounds me. The Patsy we know today gets up every week, in front of humongous crowds and arenas of women interacting with people at every turn and eating it up! You just have to chuckle at God's sense of humor. Though Patsy looks like a woman who was born to hold a microphone in her hand, there was a time when Patsy's friends and family would have surely voted her the least likely person to command a stage and endear an audience. Only God can do something as amazing as that. Where did this powerhouse speaker begin her journey from caged to free? She got up and she made that bed. Then the next day, she got dressed. She took a series of very small steps leading to a very big platform. As we do the small things God asks of us today, God begins to entrust us with bigger things.

Crisis is often just the invitation we need to cross the threshold into a new adventure. Crisis can give you the courage to try things you've never tried before. Perhaps the pride that once held you back has been thoroughly sifted right out of you. Postcrisis people, particularly those who are determined to let the crisis make them better instead of bitter, find themselves no longer protesting, "Oh, I could never do that." Instead, they greet invitations into adventure with a hearty "Why not?"

In one of my favorite lines from the movie *My Big Fat Greek Wedding,* when the brother tells the female lead—who is struggling between her past and her future—"Toula, don't let your past dictate who you are, but let it be part of who you will become." This is a profound bit of wisdom. Allow your past, even your worst failures, into your present only as part of the experience that led up to the person you are today. But do not let one experience determine who you will be tomorrow.

It's been said that there is the life you learn from and then the life you live. Many of us can relate to this concept. Take whatever lessons you can possibly glean from your past—especially from your sorrows, your losses, and your failures. Scoop up this backpack of wisdom so you can peek into it now and then for its profound lessons. Finally you can begin hiking toward your new life and new mountaintops. After all, you know who you really are now. Right?

Well, just in case you aren't completely sure, page 75 has that wonderful list of verses I mentioned earlier that can serve as a daily reminder of what God thinks of you when He thinks of you. Which is, by the way, constantly.

Our past does not determine our future.[3]

— LIZ CURTIS HIGGS

Who Does God Say That You Are?

- I am God's daughter. (John 1:12)

- I'm a friend of Christ. (John 15:15)

- I'm God's coworker. (1 Corinthians 3:9)

- I'm God's workmanship. (Ephesians 2:10)

- I can't be separated from the love of God. (Romans 8:35–39)

- I am free. (John 8:31–32)

- I am forgiven. (Romans 8:1–2)

- I can do all things through Christ. (Philippians 4:13)

- I have been blessed with every spiritual blessing. (Ephesians 1:3)

- I have Christ's mind. (Philippians 2:5–7)

6   falling into new circles of friends

*Greater love has no one than this, that he lay down his
life for his friends.*

— JOHN 15:13

When the girls in our family start talking, the boys start walking—
to find a quiet place where they can think! The chick-chat in our
family is something to stand back and behold. We have boy/girl
twins who were born at the same time, grew up in the same household, and faced the same obstacles in our family's life, yet the way
they communicate is vastly different. When I ask them how college
is going, I get lots of details from Jenn, but I'm lucky if I get a "fine"
from Jon. We have slowly lost kids from our home either through
marriage or college, but when they were all in the house, it was
quite interesting, to say the least. When we were *en masse,* there
were six girls and four boys.

First, the obvious comes to mind—yes, it is true that females in
the same family tend to get their monthly cycles in sync. Don
would often suggest that he and the boys could go check into a

hotel for a couple of days and wait out the hormonal storm in a quiet, safe place.

When it came to family meetings and/or general communication, the girls definitely added more color and drama. But when all of us girls got together, we would have amazing conversations about the facts of life, God, church, boys, music, whatever. The girls would love to ask questions, and I would try to give them age-appropriate answers. I found that my girls would sometimes talk to *my* girlfriends even more freely than they would to me. I love my ya-ya girlfriends, and so it made my heart happy when the girls would say they were going to talk to Aunt Shari or Auntie Carolyn or Auntie Laura. What a blessing to know that my girlfriends were standing by as an extra support team to our daughters. What would we do without wordy women in our lives?

Research has shown that girls say twenty thousand words a day to a boy's seven thousand. From the sounds of female bonding that often pour from our kitchen or one of the girl's bedrooms, I'd say they each are trying to get in their twenty thousand words in twenty minutes—all at once. My husband is often amazed by the mini-dramas I tell him about other gals I've just met—simply upon my return from the women's restroom. Even women who don't know each other manage to strike up temporary female friendships in the five minutes they have alone with each other, powdering noses in front of the mirror and yakity-yakking away at the same time. Don assures me that there is no conversing in a men's room. "Not even 'How 'bout them Cowboys?'" I asked.

"No, Sandi," he replied. "We're busy doing the one task we are in there for; men don't multitask at the urinal."

How boring. I'm so glad I'm not a man.

What would we girls do without our female-talking-bonding system to make us smile?

connecters r us

According to a *Los Angeles Times* article, all this girl talk isn't just fun, it is vital to our emotional and physical health! "Women are keepers of each other's secrets, boosters of one another's wavering confidence, co-conspirators in life's adventures. Through laughter, tears and an inexhaustible river of talk, they keep each other well, and make each other better."[1]

What do women talk about? Anything and everything: good reads, a great sale on shoes, the latest funny anecdote from her toddler or teen, problems—deep and shallow, and all the girly-girl stuff that tends to make their husband's eyes glaze over in signal of emotional overload.

When I get together with my ya-ya friends, I nearly always leave feeling as though I've been infused with some sort of natural mood elevator! When we all finally get our schedules coordinated and realize we have a window of time to get together, we meet and get right down to business. We know so much about each other and have so much shared history that we don't have to bring anyone up to speed. At a typical gathering, one of us will simply start in and spill her heart. Then the rest of us will ask questions and focus on that person until we're sure she's been fully comforted; and then it will be the next person's turn to vent or wail or rejoice. Sometimes all I need to say is something like, "Well, gals, I've got a photo shoot coming up." My friends will immediately know that this brings up *huge* self-esteem issues for me. So they will begin to ask me questions like, "So Sandi, how do you feel about yourself going into this photo shoot? Are you happy with the clothes? Are you comfortable with the photographer?" Then they'll start in with large cups of comfort. "Now Sandi, remember, when it's all over, it's just pictures. They can't possibly capture the real you." Knowing how hard it will be for me, they just shore me up with big doses of encouragement.

Or perhaps one of the girlfriends might begin by saying, "My son is leaving for college." We will immediately know that this brings up old issues for her because she left home at an early age and had some major struggles. We can help her see the difference between "normal" mother-son separation pain and what might be exaggerated fear because of her own past issues. But because we know each other and have history together, we instinctively know how to minister to the issues below the presenting topic.

When I am with my ya-yas I come away with two things—first, I have been heard, and second, I can be completely myself. What a tremendous gift.

The same is true with my time with the Women of Faith team. Don says that he always knows that I am going to come home from my weekends at Women of Faith a better woman. I love that. I feel it too, but it's nice to have it affirmed by those who really know you.

What's really encouraging is when we connect with each other in times of crisis and joy—it helps us to live healthier, longer lives to boot! "At least 22 studies have shown that having social support decreases the heart-racing, blood-pressure-boosting responses that humans and other social animals have to stress and the hormones it sends surging."

Men, as it turns out, do not share our feel-happy-by-talking-and-connecting system. In fact, what is good for the goose can be overwhelming to the gander. Men have other ways of soothing themselves. Like fighting wars, driving fast cars, playing professional sports—or vicariously experiencing these things by watching other guys do it on TV. It has always amused me how men can handle all sorts of physical stress, adrenaline rushes, and high-power negotiating but get weak in the knees and as lost as frightened lambs around a wordy woman in distress. That's another reason women need women friends, even if they have a great marriage—and why it is vital to keep your circle of girlfriends in good repair.

One more observation before I leave this section. After dozens of conversations with women who found themselves in an emotional or physical affair with a man, I've discovered that one of the contributions may be a lack of close female friendships. Some gals say, "I just tend to bond more easily with guys. I grew up with brothers and generally feel more at ease in conversations with men than women." If this is true for you, could I encourage you to proactively seek out women who like to do (or talk about) the same things you enjoy? Do it on a regular basis until your comfort level with them increases. Gathering and nurturing a close nest of female friends is just one more wise way to help keep temptation at bay.

even Lone Ranger needs a Tonto

The rub can happen when you, for a variety of reasons—pride, shame, mental exhaustion, independent personality—tend to think, *All I need is God and no one else.* In essence you hibernate, acting like a monk without a monastery—or even any other monkishy friends.

But cloistering yourself away from others isn't the way of true spiritual healing. God is there to fill our God-voids for sure, but He created human beings to fill our human need for human connection. In Eden, God gave Adam a human helpmate right after declaring, "It is not good that man should be alone." God did not create us to thrive without each other, so never assume that you are somehow weak if you feel you cannot make it alone, just you and God. You weren't created to do life by yourself. Most of us tend to get a little crazy when we are alone for too long: introspective or edgy or sad. Our physical bodies are wired to push us toward the cure—being with supportive people.

A confession: I tend to be a loner by nature rather than a partier. There are times when my girlfriends haven't heard from me in a while and they call or leave me a message to say, "Sandi, I've just been noticing you haven't been too verbal lately. Just missing you and encouraging you to talk and get out of yourself a bit." They know me so well. They know I need periodic get-out-of-your-cocoon pep talks.

One of the worst parts of my secret sin is that it separated me from my friends for a time. Not because of their pushing me away, but because I wanted to cover up my true heart. Before my dilemma, I appeared to be an up-front gal (though in truth I was just trying to be whatever the other person needed me to be), but during my "hiding," I found myself weaving a web of lies and wanting to be more and more isolated—in part, so no one would ask me any intimidating questions! Eventually, out of the hiding came what I hope is an approachable, honest, what-you-see-is-what-you-get kind of person.

One of the surprising reliefs of finally just telling the truth of what I'd done, come what may, was that once the hard part of confession was over, fellowship and friendship could be restored—at least with most close friends. I could start letting out my twenty-thousand words per day again with my dearest friends, even though many of those words were said with tears streaming down my face for a while. But it wasn't long before the laughter came back and with it, the healing balm of reunited fellowship.

I remember sitting in my living room with one of my friends, Carolyn, who was planning her tenth wedding anniversary celebration at the same time I was going through the end of my marriage. She was excited, and to my own amazement, I was truly excited for her. And I was sad, and she was sad for me. So we laughed and cried and rejoiced and wept. There's an old Swedish saying, "Shared joy is double joy; shared sorrow, half a sorrow." I will never forget that moment when, because of our friendship, her joy was doubled and my sorrow was lifted.

only the lonely

Back to the lonely factor and why you have to try to avoid it. According to the same *Los Angeles Times* article mentioned before, "Men and women who report loneliness die earlier, get sick more often and weather transitions with greater physical wear and tear than those who say they have a support network of friends or family." This next sentence made me wince, thinking of the devastating effects of such an easily preventable problem. "'Loneliness is simply one of the principal causes of premature death in this country,' says Dr. James J. Lynch, a Maryland-based author and psychologist who works with cardiac rehabilitation patients."[2]

In the *Healing Is a Choice* devotional, Steve Arterburn opens up with the number one choice we need to make for healing: the choice to connect with others.[3] After a crisis, or the beginning of recovery or a major transition, it is especially vital to begin creating your network of mutually supportive sojourners.

Even Jesus, in his darkest moments in Gethsemane's garden, confessed the need to have his friends nearby. If God's Son needed friends during His hour of crisis, who are we to think that we may be above needing others?

What holds us back from reaching out and connecting? Fear of rejection, perhaps. Or the thought that our dilemma or grief is so unique, there will be no one out there who will really understand or care. We know others are busy with full lives and assume they do not have time for us.

But what I've discovered is that, in general, quite the opposite is true. Most people are "God-wired" deep within to want to help others who are in pain in any way they can . . . especially people who have traversed a path similar to yours. Follow up on any leads you come across until you find someone who is able to be to you what a sponsor might be to a new member of Alcoholics Anonymous. Someone whose thirst for healing has been quenched and is now delighted to hold your hand and show you where she found the living water.

wisdom of multiple connections

A word of caution here. It is wise, when you are in especially great need of regular connection with others, to gather a variety of friends who can be available for a variety of needs and times. One newly single, and thus very needy, woman in her midfifties worked hard to make friends when she moved to a new town to start her life over. However, she also made sure she made a wide variety of connections in this time of loneliness so she wouldn't wear any one of them out. She found a neighbor who was delighted to be her afternoon walking buddy, a pastor's wife who was willing to do a one-on-one time of reading through a book and Bible study together, another gal who prayed with her over the phone, and another who was always up for a last-minute adventure to a swap meet or movie; and soon she got a job at an elementary school where she began to make friends with coworkers. Some of her newfound friends were married, some weren't. Some were old, some young. She wasn't particular about age or stage of life; she just asked God to give her one friend for each particular need in her life. Then she proactively asked around about women who might be interested in doing a variety of things that she also enjoyed, and God quickly provided. She said, "I didn't know a soul when I moved to town, other than my elderly parents. I was starting from scratch at midlife, financially and socially. I knew I had to stay regularly connected with others in order not to spiral down into the pit of loneliness, followed by the black cloud of despair."

Within a month, this wise proactive woman took charge of her own emotional health and had a stronger social network than many women who had lived in the same town for years! Within a year, she was dating the school counselor, and nine months later she was happily remarried. She refused to let the lonelies get to her, and she also ignored the statistics about the unlikelihood of marrying again at midlife. And now, she's enjoying the fruit of her courage in seeking out connections.

The Bible directs us numerous times to connect with others for a variety of reasons. In fact, I've given you a brief list of verses in the appendix. When you have some time, look them up and jot down various ways that Christians are meant to help each other during seasons of suffering and joy. You'll get a great reminder of why it is worth the effort and, yes, sometimes even the risk of occasional rejection, to keep on reaching out until you've gathered your nest of chick friends. "Connecting starts with God," Arterburn says, "but it doesn't stop there."[4]

how do you let go?

But, you may ask, what about those friends who no longer want you in their circle once you've confessed about a failure? Or what about those who suddenly disappear when you are ill or going through a devastating time? Sadly, the truth is there are usually many people who basically can't handle your particular sort of pain without overloading their brains.

In cases like this, I've found I must bless our time together and let it go. And I'm sorry this sounds like one of those hippie posters from the '70s, but it really is true: if you love someone, sometimes you really do have to let that person go. And then, if the relationship is meant to be, he or she will return.

Oh my, life has so many interesting twists and turns. I look back at a time when I wasn't able to be there for certain friends who probably needed me to be more compassionate than I was able to be with their flounderings, failures, or griefs. Now I wish I could go back to some of them and say, "I'm so sorry I didn't know what to say or do. I'm sorry I didn't understand how deep your sorrow was or how to tend to your hurts. I was young and overwhelmed, and I'd not yet been hit with my own tornado of pain. If I could do it all over again, I'd be a lot more helpful to you now."

Most of the time people who are distancing themselves really do care for you, but in some way your particular issues just bring up too much dissonance in their current understanding of Christianity, or they may trigger some personal painful responses to past events. Try to pray for them, and ask God to orchestrate a reunion and reconciliation of friendships lost, one by one, in His time. You'll be surprised as the months and years go by and "life happens" to those who once distanced themselves from your pain and they mature to a point of deeper understanding. If you don't close the window to reconciliation, you may be very surprised at who flies through that window again one day in God's timing.

Now as we look back, Don and I see that the people who had the biggest issues with us were people who were struggling in their own marriages. If it would somehow be "okay" for us to divorce and remarry, then they would have to examine their own marital pain and contemplate where it could lead. We have had some friends come to us in the last couple of years who have now gone through a divorce themselves, who said to us, "You know, I just couldn't be there for you, Sandi and Don, because I was hanging on by a thread in my own relationship and it was just too much to handle emotionally."

This past year with Women of Faith, I have been pleasantly surprised and blessed by women who have come through the autograph line and greeted me with tears. They would begin to share with me that they threw out all of my recordings because I had hurt them so deeply. I assured them that I understood full well that my choices hurt many people, and I asked for their forgiveness. They began to cry and to ask me for my forgiveness for their judgmental spirits. Such times became sweet moments of healing. And believe me, only God can do that.

I have found that the people who had the biggest, most vocal issues with me were often the ones simply struggling to survive their own lives. Because if they accepted that I'm a dedicated Christian and I still committed a major sin, they might have to change their dearly held concept that people who really love God and want to follow His ways simply don't fall into The BIG Sin Bin. Or if they accepted that a tragedy just befell someone, randomly, out of the blue, because we live in a messed up, fallen world, then it might conflict with their theology that says we can somehow protect ourselves from bad stuff happening to us—if we pray enough, read the Bible enough, or are somehow good enough. That we can keep bad things from happening to good people. Many believers resent being asked to leave their personal philosophical comfort zones in order to give the sort of compassion others need. In short, such a disaster fritzes out their brain.

You've got to find a way to bless those people, anyway, though it may take a while to do so. It helps to remember that there was probably a time when you were unable to be Christ with skin on to someone else because of where you were in your maturity or experience. So let them go and wait for God to orchestrate circumstances, over time, that may lead to a renewed connection in the future, perhaps.

Women of Faith friends

The sweetest and most surprising circle of friends God has given me on the healing side of the falling forward wall has been the Women of Faith gals who have invited me to share the platform with them. (I laughingly call them "the inner sanctum.")

I was as surprised as anyone to have been asked to share my testimony and to sing at these amazing, uplifting arena events. But then, our God is just full of surprises we never could have dreamed of or expected. Like the gift of Sam, my invitation to join the Women of Faith tour was above and beyond mercy. It was grace. It was the ring and the robe and the feasting and the dancing. The icing on the chocolate brownie. And here is how it happened.

As a recording artist, each year I meet with my manager and dream a bit about what I would like to do in the next couple of years. For a few years my dream list included working with Women of Faith, yet I somehow knew in the back of my mind it would never work. I certainly wouldn't want to "stain" all the great things they had been doing. But still, a girl could dream, right?

I received a call from my manager, Mike Atkins, one afternoon in 2004. He began by asking, "Do you have a second?"

"Sure," I said, "the kids won't be home from school for an hour or so."

He said he had just gotten off the phone with Women of Faith, and they were extending an invitation to me to join them at the National Conference in San Antonio. I must have been stunned into silence, because I remember Mike saying, "Sandi, are you still there?"

"Mike, are you sure they are aware of the mess I made in my life?"

Mike assured me that they were aware. "And Sandi, they also know a lot about God's forgiveness too. They just want you to come and sing."

I was so excited, yet a part of me was also afraid. What if this was a setup for more pain? What if when I got there, stones would be thrown in my face? But I trusted God, I trusted Mike, and I trusted that my family felt really good about my going. So I went.

I remember waiting in my seat at the bottom of the enormous arena for my turn to sing. I uttered a simple prayer: "Help." When it was my turn, I vaguely remember walking on stage and singing a couple of songs. I ended with "How Great Thou Art," and the audience was so gracious. As I walked down from the stage, the "porch ladies" (what we call ourselves when we are sitting near the front and watching each other share our stuff) were cheering and crying.

It was a bit surreal for me because I had a profound moment of identification with the woman in the Bible who had been caught in adultery. Jesus had covered her shame with His cloak. I knew Jesus had also covered me in the same way, but at this point I felt as though I were peeking out from the edges of that cloak, terrified of the condemnation that I felt would be on the faces of others.

But just as Jesus said to the woman, "Where are your accusers?" as I looked around, I could almost see Jesus smiling and asking, "Sandi, where are your accusers? You are free, you are forgiven. Go and sin no more."

And then Mary Graham walked up to the platform and waited until the crowd became quiet again. She looked me in the eyes and said, "Sandi, welcome home." What a gift. What a God.

Remember that one of the biggest blessings on the other side of the wailing wall, after a crisis or fall, is the love of friends who will be coming soon to meet you there and take you forward and ever closer to the Father's heart. Don't let loneliness sap away what little strength you may have. Proactively search out friends who can help carry you to the healing presence of Jesus when you are feeling too weak to run, walk, or even crawl.

A friend is someone who knows the song in your heart and can sing it back to you when you have forgotten the words.

— Source Unknown

7 falling into the truth

Then you will know the truth, and the truth will set you free.

— JOHN 8:32

I began this book with the story of my daughter Anna's beautiful "perfect" wedding to her husband, Collin. Like most weddings, it was a day full of joy, hope, and blissful optimism for the future, even with the little fainting spell intermission. We usually try not to bombard the nuptial couple with dire warnings of difficulties that lie ahead— it would be considered in pretty poor taste, don't you think? Besides, even if we were to warn them about how hard marriage will be at times, they couldn't hear us. They are in *love*, and love is not only blind, it is deaf and dumb. We also don't encourage the lovebirds to air all their painful memories as part of our traditional wedding ceremony, because, well, if tears are shed, most brides and grooms want them to be tears of joy. It's a day when we choose to focus on the beauty of love and the truth of God's provision for marriage.

But sometimes I wonder, what if we went to a wedding and somehow we were allowed a glimpse of the "unseen reality" behind

93

the wedding veil, so to speak? Imagine sitting down in the pew waiting for the wedding party to arrive. Up front there is a ruckus, and from a side door the groom emerges—but he doesn't look like any groom you've ever seen! Sure, he's wearing a tux, his face is washed, and his hair is spiffed up, but what's that on his back? And what's that huge thing he's dragging behind him? Yikes! It looks like he's wearing a gigantic backpack! Behind him is a wagon piled high—taller than the groom himself—with ragtag suitcases, duffel bags, cardboard boxes, and even a stray ski or two, all haphazardly bound together with rope that looks like it's going to give at any moment. You search around to make sure you know where the exit signs are in case you may need to make a quick escape. *What's going on here?*

Before you have a chance to whisper that question to the person sitting next to you, the organ strikes up "The Wedding March," and suddenly, here comes the bride. She's not only dressed in white— she, too, is loaded down with various and sundry pieces of luggage: Gucci bags slung over both arms, a Prada rucksack on her back, and in front of her, a white-rose-strewn shopping cart overflowing with everything a girl might need for her new life. Or is it everything she should have left behind?

Of course, you will never see this scenario unfold on stage in a real wedding. But as I sat in church one day listening to our pastor give a sermon based on Max Lucado's *Traveling Light*, this is the scene that was played out in our sanctuary to illustrate the baggage we carry around in life. The congregation laughed, that was for sure. But underneath the laughter was a certain recognition: *that's me.*

Not just on our wedding day, but always. Every one of us carries baggage from our past, and every box and bag we cart on our back helps to define who we are and how we behave. Those bags represent the *truth* of who we have been prior to right now, but we do not have to carry them into the future.

Wherever you are today, whatever brought you to the pinpoint of crisis or brokenness, I am going to invite you to face the truth of where you have been in the past in order to heal your future. I'm not just talking about the very recent past, but the whole boatload of baggage that you've been packing since birth.

"Whoa, Sandi!" you may be saying. "I thought this book was about falling *forward*. Why go backwards?" As I've shared throughout this book, it wasn't until I faced the truth about my own baggage that I was able to begin healing my future. Thankfully, I didn't have to unpack it alone; I had help. And I don't expect you to go it alone either.

The concept of "baggage" is particularly relevant for me because I have been traveling so much lately. As I write this, I don't think I have been home more than five days in a row in the last month. Normally I'm gone for short bursts at a time, but for some reason this is how these last few weeks have shaped up. When I get home from a trip, I have lots of bags to unpack, and they are always fuller and much messier than when I started. I usually buy little gifts here and there for Don and the kids, and of course, I don't pack as neatly when I'm coming home as I do when I'm getting ready to leave. So upon my return, my baggage is just a big fat mess.

When I got home this last time, I had a hard time unwinding from the trip, and after a day or so, I realized that my restless feelings were coming from the fact that I still had not unpacked. My bags were still full of "stuff." I knew I wouldn't feel settled until I began the process of unpacking my bags and identifying the "stuff" I had thrown haphazardly in there. I even asked Don if he would be willing to help me unload and organize. He gladly agreed. In fact, he was thrilled to help because he's a natural at neatness.

As I began to unpack, it was kind of like Christmas because I had forgotten what I had put in my suitcases. Once everything was sorted and properly put away and my luggage was empty, I began to feel the tension subside. Then it hit me—I wasn't really home in my heart until my bags were unpacked.

What baggage are you hiding behind or carrying on your back? What sacks from your past do you need to unpack? If you have been through a divorce, an abortion, or a prodigal season, that's baggage. If you were ever abused or abandoned, that's baggage. If you carry with you perfectionist tendencies, fear of failure, unrealistic expectations, or anger, guilt, shame, fear . . . all of these are pieces of luggage that need to be opened up and investigated.

What's inside those bags? This is a great time to have your journal handy and begin asking yourself some questions about the contents of those dirty old suitcases. In my situation, I needed to ask myself these questions:

- Is there someone I need to forgive (including God)?
- Is there something for which I need to repent?

- Is there anyone to whom I need to apologize?

- Is there something I need to bring out into the light of Christ's love and allow to be washed clean?

- Have I asked God, specifically, to fully heal me of each negative thing on my list?

- Is there anything I am still hiding?

You may have heard Christians say that we're not supposed to dig into the dark secrets of the past. After all, Paul wrote, "Forgetting what is behind and straining toward what is ahead, I press on toward the goal to win the prize" (Phil. 3:13–14). But I don't think he means you can just ignore the past and pretend it doesn't exist. There is healing in understanding, and I found that I needed to have a good comprehension of my past before I could really leave it at the foot of the cross.

I remember very clearly in the early days of our divorce when we were adjusting to the kids going back and forth from my house to John's. I would panic when it was time for them to go to their dad's home. Several friends offered encouragement and told me that this anxiety was normal and it would get better. But for some reason it wasn't subsiding. I knew my children were in a safe place—they have a great dad who loves and cares for them. So I sat down and started to think, unpacking the stuff in my head that was causing the cycle of anxiety, and soon realized my fear was more about *me*. I was being triggered into panic mode not because of the present, but because leaving my children with someone else for a long period of time—even their kind, protective father—reminded me of the abusive babysitting event in my past.

I remembered the terrifying loss of control I felt as a little girl because I couldn't reach my parents, who were out of town. I never even knew if they called to check on me, because the babysitter didn't tell me. Once I was able to assure my "wounded little girl within" that I was safe now, and so were my children, the panicky feelings abated.

I have found that when I have a more intense emotional reaction than seems warranted, I need to ask myself, "What pain is this triggering from my past?" It can be a bit scary, but also very healing and helpful.

Falling forward into the truth of where you've come from can be as simple as praying and journaling over the course of a few days or weeks. But if you uncover serious unresolved issues in your past, you'll benefit from the help of a counselor. Denise, a successful executive, had emerged from a reckless early adulthood to spend her thirties playing the part of the perfect wife, perfect mom, and perfect employee. She became a Christian during that time, and she remembers thanking God profusely that He'd given her a new nature—that she was washed clean and was all new in Christ. But after she hit forty, she spiraled downhill into depression, discontentedness, and disconnection. Seeking attention and affection, she had not just one adulterous affair but two. Eventually her actions became public and her life exploded—with the loss of friends, job, reputation, financial security, and even family (though the latter, miraculously, only temporarily).

Denise recalls this as her "year from hell," yet in hindsight, she thanks God for the explosion because it forced her to open up that locked-tight baggage from her past and finally, once and for all, let it go. This woman's past included so much nasty stuff (including childhood sexual abuse) that it took several months of intense work with a counselor to unpack it all. Facing the truth of where she'd been was painful! But it was only by uncovering it that she could finally understand it, discern what led to her harrowing fall, and regain hope for her future.

I caution you not to believe the old adage that time heals all wounds. In fact, as Stephen Arterburn so succinctly puts it, "Time seems to infect the wounds that are already there."[1] You have to open up those ugly scars and scrub out the poison—allowing God to heal them once and for all. If the wounds go back a long way and they are deep, you are probably going to need to seek out a compassionate, professional unpacker (Christian counselor) to help you with the task. There will be no greater gift you can give yourself or your family than a woman—wife, daughter, mother, friend—who walks free of the bags that used to bind her.

God as your credential

As you consider facing the truth of where you have been, I want to make one thing perfectly clear: eventually we have to leave the past behind. Falling forward into truth means accepting and embracing the truth of who you are now—your true identity in Christ that we talked about in Chapter 5. That baggage from the past no longer needs to weigh you down.

I have to admit, as much as I've worked to unhitch the wagonload of my past from my present, sometimes I find myself on autopilot, backing up and rehitching the load. Inevitably, I start moving through life with less energy, more introspection, and a heavy heart. All this occurs when I am tempted, in my low moments, to believe lies instead of truth. I can so easily fall *backwards* into feelings of inadequacy or unworthiness. Those are the times I have to force myself to unhook that wagonload of manure and fall forward, freely and unencumbered into God's truth.

I must tell you, I was slightly, secretly relieved to find out that my dear friend Patsy sometimes feels the same way. You see, Patsy sometimes felt unworthy of her career as a Christian writer and speaker because of her lack of official "credentials." You may have heard her speak or read one of her books and learned that Patsy dropped out of high school to marry her sweetheart. As a teenager, she had been a rebellious runaway, and later as a young mother she was overcome with numerous fears, including the agoraphobia I already told you about. And yet here she is, writing and speaking to thousands of women about the Christian life. When that diminutive dynamo takes the microphone and flashes her first mischievous grin, she has the audience in the palm of her itty-bitty hand. The women go from gales of laughter as Patsy entertains them with stories of hilarious antics followed by hysterical deadpan commentary, to wiping at a tear (she really can be as tender as she is funny) and back again. The women are glued to the edges of their seats, not wanting to miss a single word of Patsy's teaching from the Scriptures.

So you can imagine that I was shocked to find out that Patsy has, on occasion, been questioned about her lack of "credentials" and told that she should not be allowed in a public ministry!

So Patsy began asking God, "How can You let people question my credentials? Doesn't the school of hard knocks (and knees knocking) count as some sort of impressive bullet point on my resume?" She was surprised to sense an answer from God, quite different from what she expected. God asked, "Are they wrong?" Patsy responded, "Well, no. It's true. I have no educational or Bible college credentials." And God said, "But you see, *I'm your credential. That's all you need.*"

And that's the important truth about who you are today. You are fully licensed and credentialed by God. No matter what you've been through, no matter how broken or wounded you are, you are qualified to represent Christ because you are redeemed by the blood of Christ. Thank God for Jesus! Realizing this truth disarms those messages of inadequacy.

i'm feelin' it!

Do you ever have those times when your emotions lead you one direction but your intellect tells you something else? How about when God's truth says one thing but your "feelings" can't quite get with the program? Somehow you can't get your heart into what God has put in your head.

At times like this, I've wondered, *What are emotions all about, God? Why do You give us feelings if we're not supposed to follow them?* My Women of Faith friend Marilyn Meberg says, "Emotions don't have brains." So true! You could also say that the engine is the truth and the emotions are the boxcars. The truth pulls the feelings—not the other way around.

Many of us (myself included) have experienced a major fall because we followed our feelings even though they were in conflict with God's truth. Others have a hard time recovering from tragedy because of the overwhelming nature of grief—though these are natural feelings following a loss. When are feelings valued and valuable? When can it be dangerous to act on them in pied piper fashion?

First, it is important to realize that our emotions are a great gift of God, and a useful one too. We wouldn't fall in love, marry, and procreate if not motivated by that first heady rush of infatuation. We certainly would have a hard time weathering that first sleepless year of motherhood if we didn't have a fierce protective love of our little angels. We would have a harder time distinguishing evil if it didn't give rise to that unmistakable revulsion in our guts that tells us to stay away. Our emotions are usually telling us something important, but how we respond to them is where we need to use discernment.

My ya-ya sisters give me great examples when it comes to this. Just the other day I was talking with one of my friends about some of the things I've been feeling. It's hard to be away from home with my frequent travels, and sometimes my thinking gets really wacky.

I begin to feel sorry for myself and start a pity party. I invent issues and begin to obsess about them. While I was on a recent trip, Don was home holding down the fort, and kids were throwing up from the stomach flu, plus one of our girls came down with strep throat *and* mono. Yet I was taking it personally that he wasn't coming out to visit me on the road. I told you I was wacky! As I was talking to my friend Shari, she lovingly reminded me that my feelings were understandable, and that she loves me and wants me to always be honest with her, even if my emotions aren't making sense or lining up with the truth. Then she quietly and lovingly added, "But if you stay mired in those feelings that aren't based on reality, I am going to have to kick your butt."

Here's what we need to remember—and take my word for it, because I learned it the hard way: Our feelings don't *always* represent God's truth. Sometimes we have to choose to fall forward into truth *despite our feelings* about it. Often we are called to obedience directly in opposition to our feelings.

There's a wonderful line in Tony Hendra's memoir, *Father Joe*: "Feelings are a great gift, but they're treacherous if that's all we live for. They drive us back into ourselves, you see. What *I* want, what *I* feel. What *I* need."[2]

That's the key! That line really helps me understand why our feelings don't always lead us to the truth. Because, after all—I know this is hard to believe—everything isn't always about me! My feelings, however, usually are.

Another of my favorite writers, Beth Moore, says, "The nature of humankind is to act out of how we feel rather than what we know."[3] She says that the enemy knows how much we rely on our feelings, and he uses that to his advantage. To avoid the traps of the enemy, we have to learn how to behave out of what we know is truth rather than from what we feel.

But don't get me wrong. I don't think God allows us to have feelings just to confuse us or throw us off track. They're real, and I believe we have to acknowledge our emotions and validate them as real. But if the "surface" desire doesn't square with Scripture or what you know to be right, it's time to go deeper and look further to find the underlying God-given desire. A desire for romance is natural and normal. The desire to have an affair is a false way of meeting the desire. Go deeper. You long to be adored, loved, held, and cherished. How can those natural desires get fulfilled in godly ways? If we feel like our emotions are leading us astray, the answer is not simply to deny them, but to explore them, validate them, and then search for the underlying need that is not being met. That's one of the ways we choose the *truth*.

When I act purely on my surface feelings, I'm easily led astray. But when I stand firm in the truth, holding my feelings up to the light of God's Word and asking Him what my feelings are trying to tell me, I am much stronger. Occasionally, I've had to force myself to fall forward into truth that does not agree with my emotions, relying on the truth of God that has been confirmed in my heart through prayer. I have to say, I am not usually confused about truth, but I'm still bothered sometimes by feelings that do not agree with God's truth. I may never get it all figured out, but I know that God honors my obedience, and I hope He is honored *even more* when I honor His truth even though it conflicts with what I feel. Because sometimes it's hard!

In fact, our culture has a way of making feelings "king" and considering everything else as secondary. It's just another one of the ways the world lies to us. I think our character is determined by whether we act on our surface feelings or search for the truth. Virtuous character is being willing and able to act on truth—to act on our knowledge of right and wrong regardless of temptations, emotions, urges, or anything else.

So we always have to measure our emotions against what we know is truth. Falling into truth means making a commitment for today and for the future to take action based on truth, not only feelings. I know, it's easier said than done! But . . . it's the truth.

who do you say I am?

I always feel like I want to stand up and cheer when I read Matthew 16, where Jesus asks the disciples, "Who do you say I am?" Simon Peter, apparently with hardly a thought, steps right up and answers boldly, "You are the Christ, the Son of the living God" (verses 15–16).

Peter got this one right—and it was no small test. Upon this answer, Jesus told Peter two amazing things. First, this truth had been revealed to Peter directly from God Himself—it wasn't just earthly wisdom. Second, Jesus said that based on this confession, Peter would be the rock upon which He would build His church. Peter's answer to the question revealed Christ's true identity, and believers ever since have been making the same confession of faith.

The truth of Christ's identity and the truth of who God really is are the truths that outweigh everything else. When you are struggling to revive your life after a tough time, you can fall forward into the truth of who God is. Who *we are* becomes less important in the face of *who God is.*

In this world I've noticed there are the "Here I am!" people who enter a room hoping to focus the energy on themselves and the "There you are!" people, who make you feel as though they've been waiting and hoping all day to see you. The latter group is so refreshing. One of the guys on my sound crew has two of the most precious boys in the whole world. I don't see them often, but when I do, they come running to me, smiling and shouting, "Miss Sandi! Miss Sandi!" Then they hug me, and I pick them up and twirl them around. They make me feel like a million bucks. They make me realize that I want to give that feeling to the people in my life—to let them know that I'm overjoyed to see them. I want to communicate, "Hi! I am so glad you're here!" I want to get outside of my constant tendency toward self-focus and give attention to the world outside of my head. It's such a win-win because everyone gets to feel good. What's true with people is also true with prayer. When it comes to refreshing my own spirit, it helps to stop praying, "Here I am, Lord. Look at me and my problems!" and switch to praying, "There You are, Lord, all-powerful, all-loving, waiting and ready to help anyone who calls on You!"

Sometimes when I'm having trouble accepting my own failures and foibles, focusing on some of the "I am" statements of Jesus in the book of John helps me. I find comfort in knowing that all my "I am" statements ("I am a failure"; "I am unworthy"; "I am a loser"; "I am tired") are insignificant. What matters is what Jesus says *He* is.

He is the Bread of Life, and if I come to Him, I will not be hungry (6:35). He's the Light of the World, and with Him I'll never be in darkness (8:12). He is the Gate, and if I enter through Him, I'll be saved (10:9). He is the Good Shepherd who laid down His life for me, one of His sheep (10:11). He is the Resurrection and the Life, and if I believe in Him, I will never die (11:25). He is the Way and the Truth and the Life, and through Him I will get to the Father (14:6). He is the Vine and I am a branch, and if I remain in Him, I will bear much fruit (15:5).

Now I ask you, is that some amazing truth or what? It's so much easier to disregard the lies in my head when I concentrate on those incredible truths.

doing it on purpose

I hope you don't think I'm trying to make all of this sound very simple. That's not what I'm saying at all. In fact, I've found that when I'm having trouble with the whole "falling forward" concept in general, the problem is that the truth is somehow mysteriously eluding me. Lies creep in, insidiously worming their way through my consciousness, and if I don't stop them in my mind, soon I find them making their way to my heart, and then I *know* I'm in trouble!

Sandi, you're a sinner. Sandi, people don't want to hear you sing, and they sure don't want to hear you speak! Sandi, everyone knows about your Big Fall, and they're all disgusted with you. Sandi, how could you think you're good enough to be blessed ever again?

Does any of that sound familiar? I would be so happy if you could say no to that question, but in talking with women over the last few years, I've come to see that those voices are all too common. Let me tell you something right now: that's the enemy, pure and simple. And there's only one way to get rid of those voices: *Finally, brothers, whatever is true, whatever is noble, whatever is right, whatever is pure, whatever is lovely, whatever is admirable— if anything is excellent or praiseworthy—think about such things* (Philippians 4:8).

In plain English, we need to banish those nasty, untrue thoughts by replacing them with thoughts of truth and beauty and love and excellence. We have to intentionally and purposefully focus on truth. View your mind as a gorgeous garden that you work hard to seed, water, and plant with beauty. Be choosy about what you let through your garden gate. My friend Patsy (have I mentioned that I love this woman?) talks about changing her thinking when she was really battling those negative messages. She uses three steps:

1. Refuse—you have to refuse the negative messages.

2. Replace—replace them with the truth from God's Word, a line from a song, or something true about yourself.

3. Repeat—then say it over and over again until it feels true.

Intentionally read Scriptures and meditate on them. Avoid the standard fare of gossip or "woe is me" talk with girlfriends, and dive into honest, rich, and uplifting conversations. Listen to music that focuses your heart on the goodness around you; refuse to allow "junk" or fear-producing noise into your mind. Making these sorts of mini-choices every day is what it means to "take captive every thought to make it obedient to Christ" (2 Corinthians 10:5).

Whew! This probably sounds like a lot of effort, and I'm getting tired just writing about it. But there's some good news: the whole taking-thoughts-captive thing gets easier with time. It really does, and with God's strength, it doesn't have to constantly sap you of all your energy. Here's a little reality check: if you find yourself struggling long-term with focusing on truth and rejecting lies, there could be something holding you back from the freedom God wants for you. Is there a part of yourself you're withholding from Him? Is there a part of your mind that you're not allowing Him access to? Is there a secret sinful wish hidden in your heart that you're trying to pretend is not there?

I'm not trying to get in your face, but I've found that when I struggle with believing God's truth that there's usually some kind of barrier. And guess what: it's always in me. That's the hard thing about the truth sometimes! But when I open up my entire heart to God and ask Him to clean up anything negative or inappropriate, He is faithful to respond. And when I make a conscious effort to focus on the truth, He is right there helping me see it and understand.

I want to leave you with one more thought about our "thoughts." Christiane Northrup, author of *The Wisdom of Menopause*, says that

the biggest key to women's good health is *the quality of our thoughts.*[4]
Are we thinking in ways that are self-destructive, pessimistic, rooted
in the past, or stemming from lies? Or are we making the effort to
think in ways that are positive, godly, hopeful, and based on the
truth? Northrup is talking about real, physical, how-you-feel-when-
you-get-up-everyday health and its relationship to our thinking.
Her decades of work with women have confirmed what the Bible
has already taught us: if you want a healthy life, it has to start with a
healthy mind. And what is a healthy mind? It's a mind firmly rooted
in the Truth. It's that simple.

*If you do not tell the truth about yourself, you can't tell it
about other people.*

—Virginia Woolf

8 falling into your faith

We live by faith, not by sight.

— 2 CORINTHIANS 5:7

Recently I walked into a large bookstore—you know, one of those multilevel superstores. As I browsed around, I suddenly felt completely overwhelmed by the sheer volume of paper and words between those walls. Books from end to end, from floor to ceiling. Hardcovers and paperbacks. Tiny tomes and gigantic ten-pounders. Books for writers and architects and fishermen and wives and dieters and computer geeks and even singers. Thirty-thousand square feet of books!

Talk about *information overload.* I got to thinking, *What are all those books filled with anyway?* How much information do we really need—or can we possibly handle? While I'm always interested in learning new things (and I sure love a good novel every now and then!), it occurred to me that everything I truly need to know is within one book: God's Word.

Not only that, I realized that all the important things I need to know *I've already been taught.* I've read the Bible; I've read dozens of Christian books; I've listened to hundreds of sermons; I've attended years of Bible study; and I paid attention in my parents' home as they imparted biblical truth for the first twenty years of my life. With all that input, wouldn't you think I'd have applied it all by now?

Though some of you reading this may be new in faith or just observing and pondering whether or not to believe the Christian story, many of us *have* heard messages of the Christian faith hundreds, even thousands, of times. Actually, in some ways I envy those of you who haven't been surrounded by Scriptures all your lives, because you tend to look at the Bible with fresh eyes. It's not old hat.

For those of us who have grown up in a church, the downside is that we've heard the basics of the Christian faith so often that our eyes glaze over in near-catatonia when we hear generic concepts like faith, trust, prayer, and spiritual disciplines. In all fairness, I should warn you that this chapter about "falling forward into your faith" could easily be subtitled "Lessons in what you already know."

When you decide to rev up your spiritual life again after a fall or a crisis, it is important to revisit the basics—the foundational stepping-stones to spiritual growth. Here I'm going to take you through these principles with a falling forward spin, helping you to grasp old truths with some creative, out-of-the-box ways of applying them. I've outlined six key ways to fall forward into your faith after a major life calamity. These have been the areas that have helped me the most in my forward-journey, and I hope they resonate with you too.

forgive and accept forgiveness

Every tumble into the dark and dirty muck of life ends up requiring some forgiveness somewhere. If you are suffering a tragedy that was foisted on you by someone else, you may need to forgive those who were the cause of your heartbreak. If you made mistakes that led to your crisis, you are the one who needs forgiveness. If you've been a "good Christian" for years and have had some disaster hit your life, you may even feel like you need to forgive God.

So look around you. Who needs forgiveness?

In my case, even though I was the one who sinned and plunged my own life into the proverbial toilet for a while, I found there was some forgiving to do. I had to forgive my former husband, John, for not being a perfect human being. Yes, I knew it was wrong to expect that of him. But I had to cultivate a spirit of forgiveness in my heart in order to free John from any blame for my situation and to be able to take full responsibility myself. When the news of my affair first surfaced among my family and friends, I was shunned and reviled in certain circles. Later, in order to heal those relationships, I had to forgive those who expressed their very normal reactions to what I'd done. When I was in the middle of my long tumble from the spotlight and endured the public slings and arrows of judgment, I built up resentment toward all those who criticized me harshly in the media. Boy, was there a lot of forgiving to do there!

But most of all, I became vitally aware of my own desperate need for forgiveness. As my accountability group walked me through the long months of restitution and restoration, I asked forgiveness from God and from each individual who had been hurt by my actions. By the time my restoration process was declared finished, I was assured that I'd been fully forgiven.

But I still had two problems: (1) I didn't *feel* forgiven, and (2) I still had to deal with the consequences and restitution, which kept my weaknesses right in front of my face. Not a pretty sight. I had come to realize I did not *deserve* forgiveness, so I walked around carrying the guilt, not able to forgive myself for the wrongs I had done and the pain I had caused.

Then one day it dawned on me that my focus was blocking the free flow of forgiveness. Imagine that you are a photographer and you are focusing your lens on a scene in front of you. There is some old rusty, ugly junk there, and in front of that is a beautiful flowering rosebush. If you focus the camera lens on the junk, what looms large in the frame? Yeah, the junk. If, however, you focus on the rose, you see the beauty, and the junk in the background becomes a fuzzy unrecognizable backdrop.

I was focusing on my junk—my lack of worthiness to receive forgiveness. And in doing so, I was actually ignoring God's beautiful gift of His Son. I needed to shift my focus to Christ on the cross. Like the song says, "Turn your eyes upon Jesus, look full in His wonderful face."

If you struggle with forgiving yourself or someone else, remember that Jesus died for all of us equally. As you focus on the beauty of

His redemptive sacrifice, your heart wells with gratitude. Paralyzing guilt or energy-sapping grudges will flee "in the light of His glory and grace."

choose trust

Falling forward is taking a leap of faith. Remember back in chapter 1 when I told you the story of standing on the roof and falling forward off the edge into my daddy's arms? That was all about trust. I had to choose to trust that my dear dad would catch me. Stephen Arterburn writes, "You reach a point where you either move forward or you remain stagnant and miss your life."[1] How true. If I hadn't moved forward, trusting I would be caught, I'd probably still be on that roof today. (Talk about missing your life!)

Have you ever been in a corporate or retreat situation where you had to take part in "trust-building exercises"? Sometimes you're led blindfolded by someone and you have to trust they won't bash you into a wall or send you tumbling down a flight of stairs. I don't know about you, but I just hate those things! You know why? Because trusting someone else means giving up control.

That's just the worst! I hate *not* being in control. And that's exactly why trusting God is so hard. I need to trust Him for my healing, for my recovery from crisis and mistakes. It would be so much easier if I could just handle it myself! I'd love to pick up a self-help book, work the "ten steps to a better life," and be done with it. But that's not the way life works.

When I was still suffering deep pain from the mess I'd gotten myself in, I sometimes felt like it was never going to get any better. Hopelessness would wash over me, and I would sink into despair, figuring I was just going to have to live my life in the bottom of that dark pit. Simply put, I had lost the ability to trust that God had the best in mind for me. At some point, I had to choose trust again. Choosing to trust God for my provision means I'm confident He always works everything for good, even if circumstances are difficult and even though I continue to make mistakes.

But sometimes I need something else, a visual picture, to help make overused phrases like "Just trust in God" come to life. One of the most common of those dreaded corporate team-building exercises is called the Trust Fall. So when I have no idea *how* to trust God in a given situation, I think of myself climbing up on a ladder to get in position to fall, with God's strong and mighty presence waiting below. And then I mentally do the Trust Fall . . . into His arms.

When I have to perform onstage and I'm beyond tired, and I really just want, with all my aching bones and heart, to go home and put on a robe and fuzzy slippers and sleep for a week, I pray, "Lord, you know I'm out of gas. I'm going to do the Trust Fall into Your arms right now. You're going to have to give me the stamina I need to sing encouragement to Your hurting children out there in the audience today. And help me not to fall asleep standing up."

Often I fall into the lyrics of my songs, such as:

When my plans have fallen through
And when my strength is nearly gone

When there's nothing left to do but just depend on You
And the power of Your name
There is strength, there is power, there is hope in the Name
   of the Lord.[2]

And so it goes. Trusting and falling, falling and trusting, over and over again into the arms of the most trustworthy One.

have courage and perseverance

Don't you just love great stories of courage? There's nothing better than grabbing a bowl of popcorn and sitting down to watch a movie about brave people standing up to evil and winning. When the Narnia movie came out, based on C. S. Lewis's classic book *The Lion, the Witch and the Wardrobe,* our family got a chance to enjoy a "good versus evil" battle. Both the book and the movie have moments when you just want to stand up and cheer!

Like wishy-washy Edmund at the beginning of the movie, I've never thought of myself as a particularly courageous person. I probably would have been too scared to venture back into that wardrobe! In my real life, I don't jump out of airplanes, and I'm not going to climb Mount Everest. I don't even like the sight of spiders! Bravery? That's for other people, right?

Wrong.

With the amount of courage it has taken to get through the trials of the last dozen years . . . well, let's just say, some days I wished all I had to do was *just* climb Mount Everest. All the times my heart threatened to wilt under the strain of holding my head up high; all the times I wanted to give up and hide out in my bedroom forever; all the times I nearly cowered under all the lies the enemy was trying to feed me— these were moments that required me to suck it up, get a backbone, grab on to God's strength, and be a picture of courage.

Paul writes in 1 Corinthians 16:13, "Be on your guard; stand firm in the faith; be men of courage; be strong." Recovering from a life challenge is not for the weak at heart. I had to laugh when I saw a note card that said, "Put on your big girl panties and deal with it." Sometimes we need a reminder that there are times we need to be big girls and remember that we can "do everything through him who gives [us] strength" (see Philippians 4:13). There are seasons when it requires all the gumption we have just to get up every day and face the fire. But the alternative—losing heart, taking the coward's way out—guarantees exactly the opposite of falling forward. It's called sliding backward, and believe me, you don't want to go there.

I also love the verses in the Bible about perseverance, which seems to go hand in hand with courage. Persevering is all about pressing on, persisting toward your goal even in the face of weariness, dejection, or failure. Back to Narnia: remember when beloved Aslan, the lion, was killed? The children came close to losing heart, just as the disciples did after Christ's crucifixion. But they were strengthened, just as the disciples were strengthened by the arrival of the Holy Spirit on the day of Pentecost. God not only promises that the perseverance will pay off, He provides the inner strength you'll need to keep going.

We all know that courage isn't the absence of fear; it is pressing on in the face of fear. It is actually not possible to be brave unless there is something that makes you a bit afraid. Each time you persevere and act with courage, it is like building up a muscle—you get spiritually stronger. "Perseverance must finish its work so that you may be mature and complete, not lacking anything" (James 1:4). At least its nice to know, when we're going through the fire, that we're getting spiritually fit!

be thankful for everything

A five-year-old girl was asked to say the blessing at Thanksgiving dinner. Everyone bowed their heads, and she began praying, thanking God for all her friends, naming them one by one. Then she thanked God for Mommy, Daddy, Brother, Sister, Grandma, Grandpa, and all her aunts and uncles. Finally, she began to thank God for the food. She gave thanks for the turkey, the dressing, the fruit salad, the cranberry sauce, the pies, the cakes, even the Cool Whip. Then she paused, and everyone waited—and waited. After a long silence, the young girl looked up at her mother and asked, "If I thank God for the broccoli, won't He know I'm lying?"

Have you ever felt that way? Sure, we know we're supposed to cultivate a heart of thankfulness. Many of us have been cautioned since we were children to have an "attitude of gratitude." Even the secular culture has picked up on the idea of thankfulness as a buzzword in the self-help world. Oprah talks about it all the time, and on Amazon.com you can even buy a gratitude journal. But let's be honest: there's a bunch of broccoli in our lives that is really hard to give thanks for.

I'd been troubled by this for a long time. I wasn't really thankful for the self-caused explosion that rocked my world back in the early nineties. I know many women have a hard time mustering up gratitude for evils that have invaded their lives—the Internet porn that ensnared a husband, the cancer that stole a parent, the drunk driver that took a child. How can we, in our right minds, find it in ourselves to be grateful for these things?

The *Life Application Bible* explains it perfectly: "When you feel down, you may find it difficult to give thanks. Take heart—in all things God works for our good if we love him and are called according to his purpose (Romans 8:28). Thank God, *not for your problems*, but for the *strength he is building in you* through the difficult experiences of your life. You can be sure that God's perfect love will see you through" (emphasis added).[3]

Amazingly enough, by cultivating thankfulness for God's work in me as I try to glean the lessons of loss, I've even come to be thankful for the trials I've experienced. I know that through them God has made me into the Sandi I am today, a new and hopefully improved version, full of much more grace and love than ever before. Being thankful for everything—intentionally nurturing a heart of gratitude—is a way to bolster your faith on a daily basis. And (broccoli notwithstanding) I guarantee it will keep you in a better mood. It's all about how we *choose* to see the world around us. We can always find the joy in something if we just look!

pray continually

Remember that bookstore I was walking through at the beginning of this chapter? You had better believe it had a whole wall full of books about prayer. And when I took a moment to browse Amazon for Christian prayer resources, I came up with nearly five thousand books! I only have a couple of pages to work with here, so I don't think I'm going to tell you anything earth shattering about prayer. But it doesn't take long to say what I want to say: prayer changes lives.

If the muddy path you've traveled has kept you from praying as much as you'd like (or at all), I want to encourage you to start talking to God again. Even just a few words a day. It gets easier, I promise. Prayer softens our hearts. Prayer keeps us in relationship with our loving God. Prayer keeps us aware of and acknowledging our need for God.

I read once that there are three kinds of prayer we can practice, based on the example of Jesus when He walked this earth. First, there's praying without ceasing, which is our ongoing silent conversation with God throughout our days. Next, there's our "set aside" time each day for focused prayer, when we do nothing but converse with God, whether or not we choose to use words. Finally, there are the longer periods of prayer and meditation—a day or more maybe once a year—when we get away from family and responsibilities to spend extended time with God.

Now, my purpose in telling you this is not to give you more

rules to follow or to persuade you to be legalistic about prayer! I simply find it helpful to conceptualize prayer in these three ways because it gives us options and allows for our varying personalities, schedules, and seasons of life. Whatever works best for you—start there. Personally, I tend to pray continually throughout my day, because I am always singing to God!

I had a great lesson on prayer a number of years ago when Anna (my oldest daughter) was in fourth or fifth grade. She had come home after school one day and quietly said, "Mom, when you get the kids to bed tonight, can I talk to you?"

"Sure, honey," I said, and then we began to move through the afternoon and evening activities that resembled a small tornado running through our house. After I put the younger kids to bed, I called Anna, and we got some big comfy pillows from the couch, turned off all the lights, and sat down by the fireplace, and she began to share her heart.

"Mom, I am so tired. I've been playing basketball with the school team, I'm going to ballet class every night since we have that production coming up in a few weeks, and my science project is due, and I haven't even started. I'm so tired." She began to cry, and I held her for a minute.

"Honey, what do you need? Right now. What do you need?"

She said, "Mom, I just need a break." So that's how we prayed that night, that God would give her a break, a rest, a moment to catch her breath. Well, the next day she had a tournament game with her basketball team after school. She was playing with the energy that only Anna has, jumped up to block a shot, and came down hard—on her ankle. I took her to the hospital, and the whole time we were driving, I was saying to myself in a not-so-happy voice, "Well, isn't this just great. Thanks for yet another thing to stress her out." A technician took X-rays and put us in a room to wait for the results. As we sat there quietly, Anna just started laughing. And I'm thinking, *Oh boy, she has gone over the edge.* But I timidly asked, "What are you laughing about, Anna?"

"Don't you get it, Mom? God gave me a"—she pointed to her ankle—"*break!*" We burst into giggles. As it turned out, it wasn't completely broken, but very badly sprained. She had to miss the rest of the basketball tournament, which she honestly didn't mind. She got to delay her science project a few days and only had to miss a few dance rehearsals but still got to be in the production. So, God did indeed give her a "break." I love that! It still makes me laugh.

But I have to ask myself, *Would we have missed the answer had we not prayed?* Probably so. We would have seen the "break" as another stressful thing to deal with. But because we prayed and asked God to help us see the answer, we were able to see the "break" through a whole different lens.

That's what prayer does, I think. It puts us in communication with God so that when the answer does come, we can see it.

If you need a jumpstart to get you praying, grab one of those five thousand books on prayer and do a little reading. A couple of recently released books I'd highly recommend are Patricia Raybon's *I Told the Mountain to Move* and Philip Yancey's *Prayer: Does It Make a Difference?* Another older, but classic book on prayer is by Catherine Marshall called *Adventures in Prayer.* In it she explains several types of prayer, including the prayer of relinquishment (which we're going to discuss in the final chapter). And then there's Stormie Omartian's best-selling series, beginning with *The Power of a Praying Wife*. In this book, she writes out the prayers you can pray each day, which is quite helpful for women who get tongue-tied after "Dear Father in heaven. . . ." Why not visit that "wall of books" on prayer and pick one out?

purposefully grow in your relationship with Christ

A. W. Tozer wrote, "One of the greatest foes of the Christian is religious complacency."[4] He meant that we should never stop striving and growing in our Christian lives. Contentment in our worldly lives is a virtue, but contentment with our spiritual lives can be deadly. In our Christian growth, if we are not making the effort to grow and move forward, we'll fall backward. You may have read that sharks will actually drown if they don't keep moving in the water because of the unique way they get oxygen. Christians are like sharks in this way—if we don't keep moving forward, it is easy to collapse. And there's a reason I didn't name this book *Falling Backward*.

To fall into our faith, we have to intentionally nurture it. Stay away from anything that might erode your desire for God. Gravitate toward people and activities that encourage and fan the flames of your yearning for a relationship with Jesus. Read books and participate in Bible studies, but choose the ones that appeal to you. Don't feel like you have to follow the crowd or impress anyone with your selections.

Perhaps here is a good place to admit that most people experience some sort of shift in their faith after a trauma, failure, or crisis. Life crisis can precipitate faith crisis. God has not changed. The Bible hasn't changed. But your faith in God and the way you read Scripture may have changed because of your life experience. Think of God (or the Bible) as a multisided diamond. Perhaps before you stumbled and fell, you saw only one or two sides of the diamond of who God is. Maybe you felt you were able to be a pretty good girl, spiritually speaking, and you were keen on the justice of God, on obedience. Maybe you loved the black-and-white, practical qualities of the epistles of Paul.

But in your broken state, perhaps you, like legions before you, found your comfort smack in the middle of the book of Psalms, or even that tragic book of Job, where all manner of emotions are aired and soothed. At this point, God is probably balancing you out, and you'll find yourself hungry to look at the other sides of God's diamond: mercy, grace, and compassion are now all-compelling.

On the other hand, if you've been living in the world a long time—doing whatever feels good, believing whatever sounds right—and you come to faith, you will probably be starving to learn anything about the faithfulness, stability, and steadfastness of God. Your heart will be longing for boundaries and stability, and so God may spend some time revealing this part of His nature to you.

So don't be overly alarmed if your faith feels a bit shaken up after any sort of life crisis. You've probably not lost your faith at all! You are just searching for the other sides of the diamond that is God, through the multifaceted faces of Scripture.

summing up the stepping-stones

If you're ready for change after your challenge, the surest way forward is to take a long look at reviving your faith. It begins with experiencing the freedom that comes with understanding that forgiveness is about God's grace, not about your mess. Focus on that, and you'll make great strides in falling forward.

Then there is cultivating the habit of the Trust Fall into God's arms whenever a crisis comes, large or small. Next, there is a time to cry and get comforted; but gals, there's a time to put on your big girl panties and deal with it. This involves the cultivation of old-fashioned courage.

Gratitude can come, in any and all circumstances, when you realize that you can be thankful for the lessons that can be gleaned from loss, even though you cannot thank God for the bad things that happen.

Striking up a conversation with God again, especially after guilt or hurt, can feel daunting. Go slowly. Your first prayer may be, "Hello, up there. It's me again." It's a start!

Life will never get boring, and you'll never be a stagnant, bitter old woman as long as you keep growing, learning, and gleaning all you can. Stay proactive in your spiritual journey. The rewards are simply out of this world.

Faith is to believe what we do not see, and the reward of this faith is to see what we believe.

— AUGUSTINE

9   falling into serving others

*For even the Son of Man did not come to be served, but
to serve.*

— MARK 10:45

We've been through a lot together, haven't we? The journey of
falling forward has many twists and turns, winding through various
landscapes and bringing us into contact with numerous fellow travelers. Sometimes I envision this path as my own circuitous yellow
brick road—it's me and Dorothy, arm in arm, occasionally skipping
and dancing, at times cowering in fear, yet always stopping to assist
other wounded ones along the way toward that place of healing.

Those "other wounded ones" are the subject of this chapter.
Remember how Dorothy was totally focused on getting help from
the Wizard—and yet she took the time to get to know Scarecrow,
Tin Man, and Cowardly Lion and take them down the road with
her? We, too, are determinedly skipping down that bright yellow
trail, Toto in our arms, hoping to find home. And just like Dorothy,
we're going to come across others who need to find themselves and

their way back home. In this chapter I want to talk about how we can help those Tin Men and Scarecrows who cross our paths.

I love the picture of that peculiar foursome headed for Oz, because each of them had lost something precious and necessary and was looking to find it. A heart. A mind. Courage. A home. There were times in my journey when I felt as if I'd lost all those things too. My heart was broken; I felt fearful instead of brave. I'd had to leave my familiar home, and many days I felt like I was losing my mind. You, too, probably feel like you have lost something, and this falling forward expedition is all about finding it.

One thing Dorothy knew (that is all-too-easy to forget) is that we don't have to arrive at the place of total healing before pausing to assist others. I hope that by now, or sometime soon, you are far enough down your yellow brick road that you can see the glowing Emerald City looming over the hills—or maybe you are even knocking at the door of the castle already. But even if you're just two steps out of Munchkinland, I want you to know that it's never too soon to start assisting any other broken travelers that God places on the side of your path. Rather than impeding your journey, taking the time to serve others can make your travels more enjoyable and fulfilling and, in some cases, can be the key to reaching your final destination.

strengthening our sisters

Let's go back to one of our favorite biblical characters, Simon Peter, for a moment. In Chapter 4 we talked about how Jesus warned Peter that he would be "sifted" by the enemy. Jesus knew Peter was going to experience a fall—his own failure—and be devastated by it. Jesus prayed that Peter's faith would not fail even in the midst of his worst moments. But here's my favorite part: before any of this had happened—before Peter had denied Christ and experienced the shame and desolation of failure— Jesus said to Peter, "When you have turned back, strengthen your brothers" (Luke 22:32).

I love that Jesus said that! Jesus knew this failure would threaten to destroy Peter. But with this simple statement, He assured His disciple of two things: (1) He was confident that Peter would "turn back," in other words, repent and recover from the crisis; and (2) this crisis would uniquely prepare Peter to be a source of strength, comfort, and encouragement to others.

As I've thought about this verse over and over, it's as if I can hear Jesus whispering in my ear, *"Sandi, I allowed the evil one to sift you. I prayed that your faith would not fail, and it didn't. You have continued to seek Me, and you have turned away from your failure. Now, strengthen your sisters."*

Can you hear Jesus' voice speaking similar words to you?

It would be so easy for me to hole up in my house with my husband and children, keeping out of the public eye and living a quiet, private life. But those words—*strengthen your sisters*—whispered lovingly in my ear, brought me out of hiding and into the new life that God had planned for me. I don't know what He has in mind for you, but if my experience is any indication, I think He wants to use you to help other desperate travelers in search of healing.

If you've been through a tragedy or a crisis, whether large or small, whether it was self-inflicted or you're completely blameless, you have some scars to show for it. Your trial may even be so fresh that you have open wounds. God is going to heal you, but as Beth Moore says, "He will never let you be so completely healed that you forget where you've been."[1] One of the reasons He allows the scars to remain is to remind you to offer help to other broken ones along the way. Your brokenness puts you right where God wants you—not too proud, not too arrogant, but humble and ready to roll up your sleeves and get dirty.

you've been appointed

Remember back in Chapter 3 when we talked about the importance of finding those "safe people" with whom to surround yourself during your recovery from your facedown time in the dirt? You still need your safe people—but now it's time to become one as well. You are now uniquely qualified to be a servant of God, because, as my dear girlfriend Patsy says, "God uses cracked pots!"

There was a time when I honestly thought I would never be able to use my gifts to encourage or inspire anyone ever again. At times I even thought I was so far gone, God would never bless me again. Unfortunately, when Don and I married, there were Christians who told us our marriage would never be blessed.

But I've learned that God accepts us right where we are. Does He approve of the sinful choices we made? Absolutely not. Is He glad about whatever tragedy plunged you into crisis? No way. But

He always uses everything for good. From the moment we say, "God, I have really screwed up here" or "God, I am ready for your healing," He says, "Okay, let's move forward." Part of moving forward is to begin extending ourselves beyond our own lives and problems. You've had a defining life experience, and it's time to begin using it to express your love and care for others.

moving into serving others

As Dorothy knew, you don't have to get all the way to the Emerald City before stepping out to give aid to the Cowardly Lion. Hopefully, you're somewhere on that path to healing, but you can't wait until you've reached that mythical place called "there" before you start reaching out—or you'll wait forever! Your journey, fractured though it has been, has given you a greater compassion for woundedness and a deeper capacity for love. And oh, how much more grace you are now able to offer, having become of aware of the magnificent gift it really is! You are *needed* out there on the battlefield.

Pastor Greg Laurie writes: "The Christian life is not about just ceasing to do what is wrong; it's about engaging in what is right. The Christian life is not just about obeying commandments; it's about wanting to please the Lord—wanting to grow, trying to become more like Him."[2] To me, falling forward is about moving forward, which means purposely engaging in what is right. And the right thing for Christians is always to reach out in love to others. It's the logical next step.

So how do you move into a new season of embracing the wounded? For me, it started after I'd completed the formal steps of restoration as directed by my pastor and my church. Now, just because I'd finished the process, that didn't mean I felt completely healed! No, I was still an injured puppy. But as I moved forward in my life, I found certain people naturally gravitating to me. It was as if God was placing them right in front of me, saying, "Talk to this person." At that stage, I didn't have to go out searching for a "mission field." It came right to me.

Of course, I never felt I had any particular wisdom to share. I just had my own story, my own brokenness, and my willingness to listen compassionately to someone else's heart. And you know what? That was enough! As you know from your own trek down the muddy trail, having someone hike alongside you is what makes the difference between hope and despair. How different Dorothy's dance down the yellow brick road would have been if she'd done it all alone! When God opened doors for new relationships and brought me people that seemed to gain comfort from my tale, I felt incredibly honored. I would just be thinking, *Me? Are you kidding, God? Really?*

I remember one time doing an interview, and the person asked me what I thought my kids had learned through my journey. I was having a particularly difficult day, so I snapped back, "Honestly, all I think I've taught my kids is that life isn't perfect, they are going to make mistakes, and God is going to love them no matter what." Then I paused for a minute and realized that wasn't so bad. If we could really take those lessons to heart, I know I would be better for it.

One of the other things I have been amazed by has been the intensity of the letters that now come to me. Before when I tried to portray that all was perfect, I would receive shallow complimentary letters. But now the letters I get are honest about real life stuff. And because I was able to be honest about my own life, it has encouraged others to come out of hiding and share their secrets too. Wow! God really is in the restoration business. I say it often, but it's true every time: God is the God of second chances, of new beginnings. God is the God who continues to set His children free.

People tend to look at me as "that Christian singer," but I've never thought of my singing as my only ministry. I've always thought of my life as an extension of God's love and grace. So whether I'm in a grocery store or at a PTA meeting or on stage, I want to be a living testimony of God's amazing grace. I found that He began using me to speak encouragement to others as soon as I was able to lift my head from the dirt and say, "Hello." What a privilege!

My friends Greg and Becky went through a scandal that was very public in their small industry. It was a harrowing couple of years, full of heartbreak, loss of jobs, loss of friends, depression, and loneliness. Yet to their own surprise and through no efforts of their own, their home eventually became a refuge for others who were experiencing painful traumas. God seemed to lead a steady stream of injured and maimed soldiers to their doorstep—so many in fact that they finally redecorated and set aside a couple of bedrooms specifically for the casualties. Those bedrooms are seldom empty!

Becky wrote in a recent e-mail:

It really is hilarious that we, of all people, are being sought after as lay counselors. Another fellow from church called this morning and wanted some "emergency counseling" as soon as we could get together. Then last night, we were talking with a young couple about their impending marriage (yes, we are in the highly unlikely position of having been asked by our pastor—who knows our whole story—to do the premarital counseling in our church) when the phone rang and it was another single gal. "Could you and Greg possibly meet with me after church on Sunday? I'm going through some stuff, and I think you might be able to help."

We really need to hang out a shingle that says, "Unqualified, Broken Scandal Survivors Available for Hand-Holding and Free Advice."

Sometimes I really suspect they hear about the free cookies and coffee and hugs and laughter from others who've been here and are simply making up problems so they can come over for TLC. But for whatever reason they come, we are amazed at God's grace and sense of humor, and delighted they feel safe and loved here.

Don and I are going to begin a Sunday school class on blended families. It seems that the church has been getting a lot of calls lately from people who are "remarried with children" and looking for resources. So they asked us if we could help—the two people who were once the sermon topic of what *not* to do. Who would have "thunk" it?

Here's the crazy thing about all of this. When God starts bringing you others who need to be encouraged, and who need the benefit of your experience, *you're* the one who feels blessed. You realize that this opportunity to minister to sisters and brothers in need means that God has not only forgiven you, He trusts you. He wants to use you. I can honestly say there is nothing in the entire world more validating than the realization that God wants to use you again. I once heard someone say they thought one of the most profoundly good things that Jesus did was to go around touching people and saying, "You are needed." I know of few things that help the falling forward process as much as feeling useful and needed by others again.

the circle widens

Eventually there comes a time in your recovery when you may be ready to step beyond the bounds of your own circle of friends and acquaintances. It could take only weeks to get here, or it may be months or even several years. But at some point, God seems to open a door or put an inkling of desire on your heart to reach out just a little further.

But exactly what does it mean to start serving others? There's a big, wide hurting world out there. Find a place where you're needed and go for it! I'm not necessarily telling you to immediately volunteer in the church nursery or run down to the local soup kitchen (although if you want to, by all means, go for it!). There are so many ways to get outside yourself to help others who need you. Begin by looking at your natural gifts, those things you do as comfortably as breathing. Jesus loves touching the world through our natural bents and God-given talents. If you know you have a special way with elderly folks, you can volunteer to drive for Meals on Wheels or visit a nursing home. If you're a social butterfly or a great connector, look for ways to strengthen your sisters one on one or in small groups.

One friend who is great with children makes it a point to help out the young mothers in her neighborhood by babysitting their kids for an afternoon or arranging a "mom's night out." Another gal who has a heart for prayer started a weekly prayer group in her home. A woman with the gift of hospitality and a love for cooking started a "meals ministry" that provides hot meals for families in times of sickness or when there's a new baby in the house. An artist could paint a mural for the children at a women's shelter. A writer could start a newsletter or blog that is designed to uplift and connect other people in ways that bring them closer to each other and ultimately to Jesus.

In fact, once you've made up your mind to get involved in service, your problem won't be "What can I do?" It will be "How do I choose from all these opportunities?" There's always a need for volunteers. This can, at times, be overwhelming. When I feel myself trying to discern between all the voices around me exhorting me to volunteer here and help out there, I know I need to go to a quiet place and pray for God to guide me. When I have His guidance on where I should serve and how much, I can let go of any resentment or frustration and, instead, reach out to strengthen my sisters in perfect peace.

giving up the excuses

It seems we can always find plenty of reasons not to reach out and assist other hurting souls. It's all too easy for us, once we get a taste of being "out in public," to want to retreat back behind our pile of excuses and avoid serving others. It can be downright scary out there!

I remember the first few singing engagements I had several years after my public fall. I'd made sure that whoever invited me understood my history, just so there'd be no surprises to anyone. Still, standing up on stage, exposed for people to judge and condemn in their own minds, was terrifying. How I just wanted to stay home!

But fear is not a valid excuse for avoiding the service to which God has called me, and I have to say I don't think a valid excuse exists. Believe me, I've tried them all: "I don't have time; I don't have that spiritual gift; I'm still too wounded; no one wants to hear from me, I'm too much of a sinner; I'm already stretched too thin; I'm afraid of what they'll think of me; I don't feel comfortable doing that . . ."

But I believe God is telling his daughters, "Listen, precious ones. I don't require perfection; I just need all the wounded healers who are available to get out there in the world and do whatever they can, because thousands and thousands of my children are dying, starving, and much more wounded than you are. I just need people who are willing to help, not people who have it all together."

If you've seen the movie *Pearl Harbor*, perhaps you remember the young black man, a cook on the ship, played by Cuba Gooding Jr. The character was based on a real-life hero, "Dorie" Miller, who enlisted in the U.S. Navy in 1939 at age nineteen. (If you go to Pearl Harbor today, you can read and learn the rest of the story.) In 1932, FDR opened up the navy again to blacks, but in one area only; they could be mess attendants, stewards, and cooks. Basically, if you were black, you could only be a servant. Dorie was strong and soon gained renown as the best heavyweight boxer on board the ship, the *West Virginia*.

The morning of the Japanese raid, Miller was doing laundry rounds when the call to battle stations went out. He rushed to his station, an antiaircraft-battery magazine. (It was common for everyone, even a cook, to have an assigned combat task.) Seeing the magazine damaged by torpedo fire, he went above decks to help the wounded to safety.

Word came that the captain and the executive officer were on the bridge and they both were injured. So Dorie Miller went up and physically picked up the captain and brought him down to the first-aid station. Then he went back and manned a .50-caliber machine gun, on which he had not been trained, and fought back with all his might despite the unbelievable devastation around him. He became the first African American to receive the Navy Cross, presented for courage under fire.[3]

Think of all the ways that Dorie could have shrugged from battle, all the excuses he could have made for just slipping away from the horrendous scene and running for safety to protect his own life. In spite of the fact that he wasn't allowed to do anything above a cook's job in the navy, he saved two high-ranking officers' lives. Though he hadn't been trained on the machine gun, he dove in, figured it out, and began firing at the enemy. He didn't sit around analyzing why he wasn't qualified; he didn't let his fear overtake his mission. He rolled up his shirtsleeves and went to work saving lives.

Many of us simply need to give up our excuses and get to work. Jesus said that every time we do a good deed for another, we are doing it for Him. In fact, He said, "I was hungry and you gave me something to eat, I was thirsty and you gave me something to drink, I was a stranger and you invited me in, I needed clothes and you clothed me, I was sick and you looked after me, I was in prison and you came to visit me" (Matthew 25:35–36). This is the way we act as vessels of God to bring a bit of heaven down to this sin-sick world.

ministering from your misery

It's worthwhile to note that our friend Dorothy Gale from Kansas did not have to venture off of the yellow brick road to find someone who needed her help. Scarecrow, Tin Man, and Cowardly Lion just showed up right in front of her, and she most likely couldn't have ignored them even if she'd tried. Even better, they all needed roughly the same thing she did: to find courage, love, and clear-headed thinking—and to find their way back home. And that's what I've learned about the ministries to which God appoints us.

They're usually right in front of us, and they often require us to serve those who suffer in a way similar to our own crisis.

There are many women I admire who went through their own falling forward experiences and came out the other side on fire to strengthen their sisters. Just to name a few: Kali Schnieders lost her stepdaughter to anorexia and now devotes herself to educating parents about the seriousness of eating disorders. Jennifer Saake struggled through years of infertility and miscarriages and emerged to form Hannah's Hope, a ministry to women longing for children. Patricia Raybon's life turned upside down with several major crises in a row, which led her on an incredible life-changing prayer journey with God. Now she speaks and writes full-time, helping people to understand the power of prayer. Michelle Cherney was pregnant and unmarried at age seventeen, and now, years later, she is a leader of Teen MOPS ministering to girls in the exact same situation. My sister-in-law, Sandra, and my brother, Craig, have longed for years to have children, but that door just hasn't opened for them. Instead of sitting in their grief, they now work with Alzheimer's patients in nursing homes. The patients have become their children, and Craig and Sandra are some of the best "parents" I have ever known.

Is there anything more hopeful and life-affirming than being able to help someone else through a crisis that others recently helped *you* through? Whatever wound you've suffered, whatever trial you've endured, whatever failure has upended your life, you can be sure that someone else is in the same situation. Find that person, and walk with her. It could be the most important step you take in this journey of falling forward.

falling into serving others

Life becomes harder for us when we live for others, but it also becomes richer and happier.

— ALBERT SCHWEITZER

10 falling into amazing freedom

Now the Lord is the Spirit, and where the Spirit of the Lord is, there is freedom.

— 2 CORINTHIANS 3:17

Well!" thought Alice to herself. "After such a fall as this, I shall think nothing of tumbling downstairs! How brave they'll all think me at home! Why, I wouldn't say anything about it, even if I fell off the top of the house!"[1]

Alice had barely begun her adventure into Wonderland and she already had a good handle on what it would mean. If she could make it through this incredible tumble down the rabbit hole, she knew she'd have the confidence to handle pretty much anything from here on out. Now *that's* freedom. Of course, Alice hadn't yet hit bottom with a *thump,* nor did she have any idea how long this adventure would last, running here and there, chasing the White Rabbit and trying to find her way home. Certainly Alice had no inkling of how it would feel when the Queen of Hearts began screaming at her, berating her for her failings and calling for her beheading! Still, the fall itself was enough to give Alice a hint of what would come once she was back home: Freedom. Courage. A clearer perspective.

Everything I've written up until now has been leading us here, to this place where we recognize the amazing truth that this new place—down the rabbit hole, through the looking glass—can be a better place than where we were before. This new person—this *you*—is a softer, more loving, more grace-filled and thankful person than the *you* of before.

One of the most consistently voiced lessons from loss is the surprising sense of freedom that shows up in the wake of crisis. We'll spend this, our last chapter together, exploring some of these newfound freedoms and how they will help you in your falling forward experience.

freedom of boundaries

I have to admit, in the past I've had trouble with the concept of freedom as it relates to the Christian life. It's always been one of those churchy-sounding words that I couldn't quite wrap my mind around. How can we be "free" if we're subject to so many rules, precepts, and commandments? We're free from the consequences of our sin because Jesus already paid the price, but we're not exactly free to do "whatever we want," are we?

The way I like to think about this is to look at our family's two adorable pets—Brownie, a lovable mutt, and Lucky, a strange short-legged lab-hound mix. Those two crazy dogs have the run of our house, and sometimes they play outside in the yard. There's a fence around their play area that keeps them from straying, getting lost, or running in front of a car. Our dogs have freedom within the bounds of the fence, which is there to protect them. Lucky and Brownie might peer through the gate, yearning for the wide world, but they don't realize that outside the fence, on their own, they might not be safe.

It's the same with us. Within the bounds of God's protecting law, we are free. Outside of it, we are in danger of losing everything. That is exactly where I was at one point in my life.

I have come to recognize that we are always one step away, one choice away, from falling. The more I understand what I'm capable of, the more amazing God's grace is to me and the more I appreciate commonsense boundaries as ways to protect me from myself. I try not to look at anybody else's mistakes and say, "I could *never* do that." Whoa—red flag! If I *think* I could never fall down a particular sin ditch, then I won't set up safeguards in my life against it. We might think, *My puppy is so obedient he'll never leave the yard,* we'll neglect to build a fence—and before you know it, that well-behaved puppy may be out in the middle of the street.

Back in the '60s, the hippie era brought with it the concept of "free love" and "open marriages" that proved to be a societal, experimental disaster. A marriage without boundaries bred the worst kinds of insecurity. It wasn't long before the pendulum swung back in the direction of commitment and traditional family units, where mutual marriage vows gave longed-for stability and safety to relationships.

In that same era there were failed experiments in permissive parenting where kids ran wild and were ultimately found to be less secure than children from homes with lots of love bolstered by firm rules that were given in order to create order and peace. Then there was every teacher's nightmare: the concept of open public school classrooms without walls. (Eventually, in sheer desperation, teachers ended up building makeshift walls out of boxes and old textbooks to recreate some semblance of order and help manage the endless stream of distractions from all the classrooms in session around them. Talk about an ADD disaster!)

Our freedom-loving society discovered something surprising. Freedom without boundaries did not lead to positive self-image or kinder ways of relating or more relaxed citizens. Instead, the imbalance led to chaos, insecurity, and fear. There has to be a balance of freedom within some basic confines for human beings to function at their best.

Most of us who have survived a failure can admit that at some point, we got off balance in our yearning for freedom without the wisdom of boundaries. Perhaps married people failed to put boundaries around meeting alone with the opposite sex. (This is a boundary that Don and I agree to have firmly in place in our marriage, now that we both are more aware of temptation's pull.) Or perhaps we rationalized our way into addictions as we argued for our "personal freedoms," but the result of our freedom cost us and others dearly. Many young women bought into freedom of choice to be sexually active and, because they didn't put boundaries around their own bodies, ended up wounded, alone, diseased, pregnant, feeling used, and surprised at how costly "free sex" turned out to be.

A wise parent corrals a young child out of love and prefers not to let their little darling freely expand his horizons by inserting a metal coat hanger into an electrical socket. The cost of that particular freedom is too high. However, wise parents do allow choices within boundaries. "Do you want to play with these plastic blocks or read a book?"

God, our Father, treats us the same way. He only gives us boundaries to keep us from making the sorts of poor choices that could lead to consequences He knows would be too costly to our souls. But within boundaries, God gives us a huge variety of choices. Even in Eden, though Adam and Eve focused on the one tree they were not supposed to touch (oy vey!), God had made sure they had a huge variety of delicious fruits and vegetables to choose from each day.

After learning the hard way that freedom needs to be balanced with boundaries, most of us stumblers have a new appreciation for God's loving wisdom in establishing guidelines with our best interest in mind. There's freedom in realizing this at the deepest heart level.

freedom of surrender

As Alice plummeted down the rabbit hole, she seemed to grasp right away that things in her life would not be the same after this. She gave up that expectation and immediately embraced the newness surrounding her. She found things "curious and curiouser," yet she went with it. She didn't fight it. She gave up expecting things to be as she had always known them to be. And with that giving up came a freedom to explore her new life.

In my own life, as I was experiencing my fall from grace and then trying to recover from it, I found I couldn't move forward until I gave up my own expectations from the past. You see, in the midst of my pain, I was clinging tightly to what I already knew. I was a Christian singer. I recorded albums and won awards and performed concerts. People liked me and respected me. I had to let all of it go in order for God to teach me something new.

One of my favorite old hymns is "I Surrender All." The words are simple, and even as a child, I always loved imagining I was singing straight to Jesus, "I surrender all, I surrender all. All to Thee, my blessed Savior, I surrender all." It felt like such a powerful statement of giving my whole self to Christ—body and soul! And even though at such a young age I didn't fully understand what *surrender* was, I knew it was something I wanted to do. The song hinted to me that if I could only do it—if I could really just *do* what the song says—that the joy and the reward would be something so amazingly wonderful that it would be worth every bit of sacrifice it took.

The hope and the joy in "surrender" just took my little-girl breath away. And yet, for years, my life was characterized by an incomplete surrender to Him. I might have been devoutly reading Scripture, and attending church, and doing my best to love others and obey God's precepts, yet there were parts of me that were not surrendered—parts of my heart that seemed too dear to share, too personal to relinquish.

In truth, it was this incomplete surrender that led me down the garden path to a gigantic ditch—into which I promptly fell. Even now I continue to struggle with areas of my life that need to be surrendered to God. It is, like the title of another of my favorite children's movies—the *Neverending Story.*

It is interesting how God brings each of us to the point of full surrender. Catherine Marshall, the author of *Christy* and other classic Christian books, is known for having coined the term "the prayer of relinquishment." She learned of the power of surrender, or the prayer of "I give up," when she had done all she knew to do, exhausted all medical resources, and prayed all the prayers she knew to pray during a long illness. Finally, she simply prayed, "I'm tired of asking. I'm beaten, finished. God, you decide what you want for me the rest of my life." Tears flowed. She had no faith as she had understood faith to mean (a sort of "trying really, really hard to believe" kind of faith).

To Catherine's surprise—after she prayed the prayer of surrender, or relinquishment, or "I give up to whatever You want," peace entered. God touched her deeply, and in her case, this surrender actually started her own physical healing.[2]

In a fascinating follow-up story years later, film producer Ken Wales, a good friend of Catherine's, had a dream to make a movie out of her best-selling novel, *Christy.* When Catherine died, he felt strongly that making this dream a reality would be a way to honor his dear friend. So Ken put his whole heart and most of his money into the project, but when the stock market crashed in the 1980s, everything fell apart.

Obstacle after obstacle stood in his way. Ken writes, "By 1993 I had reached a turning point. For 17 years I had been consumed by *Christy*, and nothing had worked out." Finally, he was ready to give up the struggle and place the dream in God's hands.

Ken prayed sincerely, "Father, I'm simply out of gas. *Christy* has to be totally in your hands. And whatever comes out of this, I'm prepared. I no longer have to have my dream." Ken explains, "Through that kind of surrender, which Catherine Marshall wrote much about—the prayer of relinquishment—God often meets us. Just a few days later, CBS called again. This time, when they asked about a *Christy* TV series, I knew it was right."[3]

It is interesting how often surrendering to God is precipitated by hitting a wall in our attempts to orchestrate our own lives. Surrender is sincerely saying to God, "Lord, I'm out of energy. Have your way in this area of my life. I am choosing to let go of my expectations about how it turns out. I need to stop striving and I need to rest! I am giving this to you—please take over."

Though the hymn says, "I surrender *all*"—it is nearly impossible to surrender every part of yourself and your life at one time. It's more like a lifelong journey of small surrenders as circumstances present themselves. I've found that when I practice the small surrenders, the bigger ones come quicker, with less hanging on. The more I let go of my cherished delusions of having control over my life, the easier it is for me to surrender. The good news is that peace enters when the struggle for control is over. Freedom arrives when the last bit of self-sufficiency departs.

In order to turn the corner to freedom, I had to learn this lesson the excruciatingly hard way. I had to relinquish my right to everything, my expectation of anything. I had to say, "Whatever, Lord," and really mean it. I remember the exact moment it happened. (Forgive me if you've heard this story before, but I think it's worth relating. It was one of the biggest turning points of my life.)

It was during the time when I was separated from John, my first husband, and we lived in different cities. I was in love with Don, and certain people in my life had an idea of what was going on, but I hadn't totally confessed the entire story to anyone. I was trying to preserve my career, my reputation, and my squeaky-clean image and still living a life of secrets. I had become aware that *Christianity Today* was going to print a tell-all article the following month, and there was nothing I could do to stop it. I just felt myself falling apart.

I was traveling home and trying to make it there for the birthday party of one of my children. There was a snowstorm, and I ended up stuck in the Cleveland airport, unable to get a flight out. I was completely stressed about missing the party, about the *Christianity Today* article, and about the fact that my life was spinning out of control. I reached the end of myself right there, splayed on the floor near the boarding gate with my luggage all around me. I pulled out my cell phone, called my pastor, and said, "You know what? I'm *done*. I'm done trying to play catch-up. I'm done hiding. I'm done trying to save my career. I'm done caring about my reputation. I don't care who knows about me anymore. I don't care. I just want to be clean before the Lord." It was a liberating moment for me.

Pastor Jim talked to me for a few minutes and clarified with me what I was saying. Yes, I was really handing it over to God. Yes, I was really fine with it if I never sang again, if I never made another record, if I never saw Don again. I gave it all up.

From the moment I did that, this feeling of amazing freedom came over me because I no longer had to hide. I no longer had to pretend to be something I wasn't. I was done troubleshooting, done doing damage control, done trying to hide my sin. I knew I was going to be okay even if I never sang another song or made another record. Like the line from the song "Me and Bobby McGee" says, "Freedom is just another word for nothin' left to lose." There's truth in that. I had nothing left to lose but my grip on what was already gone. I was in God's hands now. That was the most freeing moment of my life.

freedom to live openly in the light

If you had told me ten years ago that I'd be writing books, speaking to women, and even performing concerts again, I wouldn't have believed you. Or I might have thought it only would have been possible if I'd somehow managed to keep my sins hidden. Now I try to imagine it—living life carrying around this dark secret—and I cringe at how awful that would be. Living in the light and refusing to be afraid of the truth means I no longer have to pretend.

Being the same person inside and out, acting and behaving according to what we believe—this is freedom! There is no more dissonance between who I really am and who I present to others. I am free to be myself! I can be a person of integrity and character—flaws and all, admitting openly that there was a bad chapter in the story of my life, because I'm not trying to pretend I'm anything that I'm not.

You might be amazed at how freeing it is to lose your reputation. Devastating, yes. I have to admit, it has been one of the most painful experiences of my life. But I'll tell you what—it has freed me from worrying that I might lose my reputation! Been there, lost that, and I'm still breathing. When you survive what you once thought would be an insurmountable loss, you realize that you and God can face just about anything together. I have found that being real, being yourself, is a lot more attractive to others than trying to impress them anyway.

It has forced me to rely not on my own reputation but on God's. It's been made painfully clear that I am not perfect—but *He* is. I can't atone for my sins—but *he* did. As I talked about back in Chapter 7, God is the only credential we need, and that frees us from worrying about our own lack of certifications, diplomas, and degrees.

To find ultimate freedom, you begin to let who you really are inside shine to the outside world. The world becomes a sort of "come as you are" party—where you are happy to show up just as plain old you: a beloved pilgrim, very much in progress.

freedom to be who you are becoming

Back in Chapter 1, I painted a picture for you of all of us—thousands of women—with scarlet letters on our chests. At first we thought those *A*'s stood for all the sin and brokenness we carried with us, but then we realized that the *A* represented *atonement*—the completely amazing idea that Jesus has washed us clean of our sins, dressed our wounds, and made us whole again. That's the image I want to leave you with, because to me, there is no greater picture of freedom.

There are several places in Scripture where the color "scarlet" is mentioned, and it always carries with it more weight than just any old color. In fact, in the book of Joshua there is a story in which the color scarlet actually represents freedom. The Israelites are about to take down the city of Jericho. Rahab, a prostitute in Jericho, has put herself in danger by assisting two Israelite spies. In return, the spies promise that although the entire city of Jericho will be destroyed and every man, woman, and child will be killed, Rahab and her family will be spared.

But there needs to be some sort of signal on the outside of Rahab's house so that when they come back to destroy the city, they'll know which house to spare. Rahab was told to tie a *scarlet cord* in her window. The scarlet cord saved Rahab and her family.

Freedom.

Interestingly, the fact that Rahab was saved from the slaughter on Jericho would turn out to be significant. Apparently she stopped living the life of a prostitute and got married. She bore children, and a few generations later, none other than Jesus Himself descended from her.

The reason I love this story so much is because Rahab's *freedom*, symbolized by the scarlet cord, came from her obedience and her decision to turn her life around. It no longer mattered to God that she'd been living a sinful life. As Liz Curtis Higgs says, "With God, it isn't who you *were* that matters; it's who you *are becoming*."[4]

Who are you becoming? Aren't you excited to find out what God has up His sleeve for you next? Hang up that scarlet cord of freedom on the doorpost of your past. Then get ready for the new thing God is going to do in and through you!

final thoughts

Because of the path I've traveled—from perfect christian girl to really messed up sinner to redeemed child of God—I've really found myself wanting to talk to other women about their own struggles. I've met women who've failed in their lives or abandoned their faith or have been angry at God. I've met women who didn't make choices that were wrong yet still seemed to move through life with the filter of "I'm worthless" and "I'm not beautiful" and "I don't matter."

I've found myself wanting to say to women—to you—"Please, learn from what I've gone through!" If you're stuck in some way, you have a decision to make. You can't stay stuck any longer, so you have to fall off that fence one way or the other. Are you going to believe the past lies? Or are you going to trust that your dad will be there to catch you, and just go for it? I've been there. I had to say, "God, I don't know if You love me or not. But it takes as much faith to believe You *don't* as it takes to believe You *do*. So I'm going with what has seemed to work for other people. I'm going to literally fall forward on that side of the fence. I don't know if You love me or not, but I'm going to choose to believe You do and act as if I do. So here I come, Father. Catch me!"

My pastor was clear when Don and I came to the point of putting closure on our past: there is an *end* to the restoration process. What a concept! There came a point when he encouraged us to stop apologizing and start living; to quit looking behind us and focus on today and tomorrow. To quit holding the lowly "I made a bad mistake" posture and hold our heads up again as fully restored kids of the King.

Our church helped us as we made a choice to step into the river of joy. They do not bring up the past. They treat us the same way they treat every married couple in our church. They love our blended bunch of kids. They gave away our "sickbed" a long time ago and encouraged us to get our minds off our past and onto the tasks that would bring a bit of heaven down to earth again—serving others in need.

We're falling forward into a future that looks so bright we may have to buy stock in shades.

Why don't you grab a pair of your snazziest Ray-Bans, Oakleys, or Walgreen knockoffs, smile broadly at your future, and jump headlong into your Father's arms?

falling into amazing freedom

Freedom is not something that anybody can be given. Freedom is something people take, and people are as free as they want to be.

— JAMES BALDWIN

11 falling into further study

questions for reflection or discussion

1. What does *perfect* mean to you, and how has your definition changed? (Ch. 1)

2. Imagining yourself among the women wearing large scarlet letters on their chests, what letter would you be wearing, and what does it stand for? (Ch. 1)

3. Do you relate more to the prodigal son or the older brother in the parable? Has that changed recently? (Ch. 2)

4. Can you identify a time when you first began to falter? What were the signs? What happened? (Ch. 2)

5. Who are your safe people, and how have they helped you? (Ch. 3)

6. In what ways has your view of God changed through your journey? (Ch. 3)

7. How might you benefit by refusing or neglecting to "get well" after this crisis? (Ch. 4)

8. What are some of the conscious choices you've had to make in order to pursue healing? What have been the results of those choices? (Ch. 4)

9. In what ways has your view of yourself changed in the course of this crisis and recovery? (Ch. 5)

10. What blessings have you seen in your life recently? Is it difficult to identify them? (Ch. 5)

11. What kinds of changes have occurred in your friendships? How have you adapted? (Ch. 6)

12. Have you been tempted to isolate yourself, or have you found yourself isolated by circumstances? If so, how have you dealt with this? (Ch. 6)

13. As you look honestly at the baggage you may be carrying, are there any surprises? How are you choosing to deal with the baggage? (Ch. 7)

14. What are your thoughts on the question of feelings versus truth? Do you think your feelings generally represent truth or do they lead you astray? (Ch. 7)

15. Where are you with forgiveness in your life? Do you have trouble forgiving yourself or accepting God's forgiveness? Are you having trouble forgiving someone else? What can you do about it? (Ch. 8)

16. What is most difficult for you: being trusting, being courageous, or being thankful in everything? How has this impacted your recent journey? (Ch. 8)

17. What kinds of opportunities have fallen across your path to encourage others on their journeys? How have these affected you? (Ch. 9)

18. Have you taken proactive steps outside your own circle to serve others? If so, what does this do for your own healing process? If not, might you consider it? (Ch. 9)

19. Where are you in your surrender to God? Are you aware of holding anything back? If so, why do you think you are doing it? (Ch. 10)

20. How do you experience greater freedom because of the path you've been on? What makes you free? What threatens your freedom? (Ch. 10)

sandi's bookshelf

Here are some wonderful books to help you keep falling forward.

Brennan Manning: *Ragamuffin Gospel* and *Abba's Child*

Philip Yancey: *What's So Amazing About Grace* and *The Jesus I Never Knew*

Henri Nouwen: *Life of the Beloved* and *The Return of the Prodigal*

Patricia Raybon: *I Told the Mountain to Move*

Stephen Arterburn: *Healing Is a Choice*

Greg Laurie: *The God of the Second Chance*

Beth Moore: *When Godly People Do Ungodly Things*

Jerry Bridges: *The Pursuit of Holiness*

R. T. Kendall: *Total Forgiveness*

Carol Kent: *When I Lay My Isaac Down*

scriptures to help you fall forward

scriptures that remind us to connect with others

In Christ we who are many form one body, and each member belongs to all the others. (Romans 12:5)

There should be no division in the body, but that its parts should have equal concern for each other. (1 Corinthians 12:25)

Encourage one another and build each other up, just as in fact you are doing. (1 Thessalonians 5:11)

Be completely humble and gentle; be patient, bearing with one another in love. (Ephesians 4:2)

Carry each other's burdens, and in this way you will fulfill the law of Christ. (Galatians 6:2)

verses to remind you of your true identity

As the Father has loved me, so have I loved you. Now remain in my love. (John 15:9)

Now if we are children, then we are heirs—heirs of God and co-heirs with Christ, if indeed we share in his sufferings in order that we may also share in his glory. (Romans 8:17)

Don't you know that you yourselves are God's temple and that God's Spirit lives in you? (1 Corinthians 3:16)

He predestined us to be adopted as his sons through Jesus Christ, in accordance with his pleasure and will—to the praise of his glorious grace, which he has freely given us in the One he loves. (Ephesians 1:5–6)

In all these things we are more than conquerors through him who loved us. (Romans 8:37)

verses to remind you that you're forgiven

Therefore, there is now no condemnation for those who are in Christ Jesus, because through Christ Jesus the law of the Spirit of life set me free from the law of sin and death. (Romans 8:1–2)

In him we have redemption through his blood, the forgiveness of sins, in accordance with the riches of God's grace that he lavished on us with all wisdom and understanding. (Ephesians 1:7–8)

Be kind and compassionate to one another, forgiving each other, just as in Christ God forgave you. (Ephesians 4:32)

As far as the east is from the west, so far has he removed our transgressions from us. (Psalm 103:12)

"Come now, let us reason together," says the LORD. "Though your sins are like scarlet, they shall be as white as snow; though they are red as crimson, they shall be like wool." (Isaiah 1:18)

verses to remind you of your freedom in Christ

If the Son sets you free, you will be free indeed. (John 8:36)

You have shattered the yoke that burdens them, the bar across their shoulders, the rod of their oppressor. (Isaiah 9:4)

But now that you have been set free from sin and have become slaves to God, the benefit you reap leads to holiness, and the result is eternal life. (Romans 6:22)

Now the Lord is the Spirit, and where the Spirit of the Lord is, there is freedom. (2 Corinthians 3:17)

Focus on the Family
1-800-A-Family
www.family.org

New Life Ministries
1-800-NEW-LIFE
www.newlife.com

Crossroads Christian Counseling
719-395-4673
www.crossroadscounseling.net

This counseling retreat center set in the small mountain town of Buena Vista, Colorado, features brief, intensive treatment. It is staffed by believers with excellent counseling credentials. Several of my friends have gone there for intensives and have come back with glowing reviews of the help they received. There is real value in doing intensives over a short period of time, getting the help you need immediately, rather than dragging out the process for a year or more.

Remuda Ranch

1-800-445-1900

www.remudaranch.com

Remuda Ranch provides biblically based intensive inpatient and residential programs for women and girls suffering from eating disorders and related issues.

Life Coaching and Life Planning

Nearly all life coaching is done via telephone. Life planning is always done in person, often in intensive sessions of eight hours or more.

Carol Travilla and Joan Webb: www.intentionalwoman.com

There is a list of certified life planners at

http://www.purposedrivenlife.com/pathfinders/lpfacilitators.aspx

These are Christian life planners certified under the Tom Paterson process affiliated with Rick Warren's Saddleback Church.

There is a list of Christian coaches at

http://www.christiancoaches.com/

Christopher McCluskey is a Christian coach who teaches/trains other Christian coaches. His Web site is full of useful information. http://www.christian-living.com/

notes

CHAPTER 1

1. Henri Nouwen, *Life of the Beloved*, (New York: Crossroad, 1992), 48–49.

2. *Spiritual Renewal Bible* (Wheaton: Tyndale, 1998).

3. Sheila Walsh, "Who Are You?" This article first appeared in *Leadership Journal magazine*, Summer 2002. Reprinted by permission. www.christianitytoday.com.

CHAPTER 2

1. *The Merriam-Webster Dictionary* (New York: Pocket Books, 1974), 259.

2. Henri Nouwen, *Return of the Prodigal* (New York: Image Books/Doubleday, 1994), 80–81.

CHAPTER 3

1. Donald McCullough, *The Wisdom of Pelicans* (New York: Viking Press, 2002), 98.

CHAPTER 4

1. Joyce Meyer, *Beauty for Ashes* (Nashville: Warner Faith, 2003).

2. T. D. Jakes, *Creative Pastor's Blog*. See section on 2006 C3 Conference and T. D. Jakes's *10 Commandments of Christian Leadership* (Commandment #6: "Thou Shalt Make Ministry Out of Your Misery") http://cp.blogs.com/cp/2006/01/index.html.

3. Margery Williams, *The Velveteen Rabbit* (New York: Avon, a division of HarperCollins, 1999), 5.

4. Beth Moore, *Jesus the One and Only* (Nashville: Broadman & Holman, 2002), 285.

5. Ibid.

6. The Quotations Page, *Quotations by Subject*, http://www.quotationspage.com/subjects/reputation/.

CHAPTER 5

1. Lisa Schneider, *Joan Didion: Grief Becomes a Part of You*, Beliefnet.com. http://www.beliefnet.com/story/190/story_19007_1.html.

2. Charles Spurgeon, *Lectures to My Students* (Grand Rapids, MI: Zondervan, 1979), 154.

3. Liz Curtis Higgs, *Bad Girls of the Bible* (Colorado Springs: Waterbrook, 1999), 166.

CHAPTER 6

1. Melissa Healy, "Science confirms that women reap health benefits from friendships," *Los Angeles Times,* May 19, 2005. Used by permission. All rights reserved.

2. Ibid.

3. Stephen Arterburn, *Healing Is a Choice* (Nashville: J. Countryman, 2005), 11–12.

4. Ibid., 18.

CHAPTER 7

1. Stephen Arterburn, *Healing Is a Choice* (Nashville: J. Countryman, 2005), 53.

2. Tony Hendra, *Father Joe* (New York: Random House, 2005), 90.

3. Beth Moore, *When Godly People Do Ungodly Things* (Nashville: Lifeway, 2003), 19.

4. Christiane Northrup, *The Wisdom of Menopause* (New York: Doubleday, 2003), 65.

CHAPTER 8

1. Stephen Arterburn, *Healing is a Choice Devotional* (Nashville: J. Countryman, 2005), 99.

2. "In The Name of The Lord," music and lyrics by Sandi Patty and Gloria Gaither. River Oaks Music and Gaither Music Studios. All rights reserved.

3. *Life Application Study Bible*, New International Version (Wheaton: Tyndale and Grand Rapids: Zondervan, 1991), 2139.

4. A. W. Tozer, *The Root of Righteousness* (Camp Hill, PA: Christian Publications, 1986).

CHAPTER 9

1. Beth Moore, *When Godly People Do Ungodly Things* (Nashville: Lifeway, 2003), 105.

2. Greg Laurie, *The God of the Second Chance* (Wheaton: Tyndale, 2002), 59.

3. National Geographic Website, "Pearl Harbor." http://plasma.nationalgeographic.com/pearlharbor/ngbeyond/people/index.html.

CHAPTER 10

1. *Lewis Carroll: The Complete, Fully Illustrated Works*, deluxe ed. (New York: Gramercy, 1995), 6.

2. Catherine Marshall, *Adventures in Prayer* (Grand Rapids, MI: Chosen Books, a division of Baker Publishing Group, 1975), 52.

3. Ken Wales, "Christy: In the Fullness of Time," 1995, http://members.tripod.com/~Constance_2/fight.html.

4. Liz Curtis Higgs, *Bad Girls of the Bible* (Colorado Springs: WaterBrook, 1999), 165.